Vintage
Style

First published in 2020 by Redshank Books ∎ Copyright © Zoey Goto ∎ The right of Zoey Goto to be identified as the author of this work has been asserted in accordance with the Copyright, Designs and Patents Act, 1988 ∎ ISBN 978-1-912969-10-4 ∎ All rights reserved. No part of this publication may be reproduced, stored in any retrieval system or transmitted in any form or by any means, electronic, mechanical, photocopying, recording or otherwise, without the prior written permission of the copyright holder for which application should be addressed in the first instance to the publishers. No liability shall be attached to the author, the copyright holder or the publishers for loss or damage of any nature suffered as a result of reliance on the reproduction of any of the contents of this publication or any errors or omissions in its contents ∎ A CIP catalogue record for this book is available from The British Library ∎ Photographs by Zoey Goto ∎ Design by Helen Taylor ∎ Printed in the UK by Severn.

Redshank Books, Brunel House, Volunteer Way, Faringdon, Oxfordshire SN7 7YR

Tel: +44 (0)845 873 3837

Redshank Books is an imprint of Libri Publishing.

www.libripublishing.co.uk

Vintage Style

Zoey Goto

*INSIDE THE DAPPER
WORLD OF RETRO
ENTHUSIASTS*

REDSHANK
BOOKS

Dedicated to my daughters
Summer and Indiana,
who also love a charity
shop rummage.

Contents

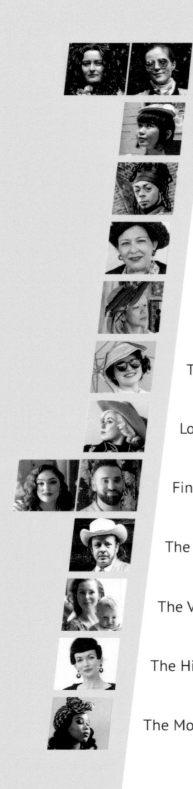

Our love affair with the high street is slowly fading, with predictions that second-hand fashion will overtake fast fashion within the next decade. This movement away from mass-produced clothing has been largely driven by millennial consumers – motivated by eco-concerns, financial restrictions and a desire to express more individuality through their styling and garments. Technology has also been a game-changer, with apps and websites eliminating the need to riffle through dusty piles of clothing to bag a bargain.

Since I could dress myself, I've always worn some element of second-hand clothing but the reasons behind this have shifted over time. What was initially about dressing creatively and a lack of funds has in recent years been upstaged by environmental concerns. The human cost of exploitative sweatshops, impact of fast fashion on the natural world, including carbon emissions and water pollution, teamed with the relentless quest for the new, with some high street brands releasing entirely new collections every fortnight, seemed unsustainable and out of step with modern thinking. In Britain alone, it's estimated that every year we throw away clothing worth £12.5 billion, taking up 300,000 tonnes of landfill space.

So around three years ago, armed with the idea that there's probably already enough clothing out there in the world, I decided to try out a more circular fashion model. I stopped buying virgin fabrics, gave away my unwanted clothing and re-styled what was left of my wardrobe, jazzing it up with charity shop and eBay finds. I also started to clock the stylish vintage enthusiasts around me who were reappropriating old clothing and styles, bringing them into the contemporary in new and interesting ways. This book was born out of this fascination.

The vintage lovers in this book don't share a geographical location, living everywhere from Hollywood to Brighton, or from Sicily to Sheffield. They also don't share an interest in the same specific era, as the timespan of the periods being referenced spans from the 1640s to the 1980s. Whilst some revel in the sociable vintage scene and its sense of community, for others it is most definitely a solo pursuit.

The stories are as diverse as the wearers themselves, although common threads did weave their way through many answers, highlighting an interest in a low-consumption lifestyle, a feeling of being outside the mainstream, and the idea of the outer appearance finally matching how the wearer felt inside. Often, the interest in vintage was sparked in childhood by a wonderfully memorable movie or musician, or just the experience of second hand shopping with relatives as a kid.

For me personally, the universal thing that binds all the vintage revivalists who kindly allowed me into their world, is that they're all at the more intense end of retro style. Take Tracy's Tiki-tastic Palm Springs palace, where every single object has been so carefully curated, or the spangly brilliance of Texas Joe's Western wear, which brightens up his London neighbourhood on a grungy day – these are the people who are taking vintage style to the extreme, and therefore most interesting, end of the fashion spectrum.

Special thanks to Helen Taylor for designing this book so beautifully, and to Celia Cozens for her hard work editing *Vintage Style*.

Foreword by Wayne Hemingway MBE: Designer, co-founder of the iconic label Red or Dead and organiser of Vintage by the Sea

I was born into a working-class household where nothing went to waste and mum was forever making clothes. The tipping point was going to see David Bowie in Blackburn in 1973 when I was 12 – I was blown away by his style and wanted to look like him. With no money, it was a case of DIY – charity shops, army surplus and a bit of creativity with scissors. Through my teens second-hand became a way of life. It allowed me to be an individual, creative and still have enough money to go see bands, go clubbing, watch Blackburn Rovers and buy records.

When my wife, Gerardine, and I started selling second-hand clothes on Camden Market 30 years ago, the term "vintage" wasn't used in association with anything except wine and cars. And I still call my clothes second-hand. But I suppose that what separates a vintage frock from a second-hand H&M top is design quality – vintage items stand the test of time.

As my kids have grown into adults and I have seen them and their friends mix and match clothes from previous decades, have seen them "borrow" from Gerardine and my wardrobes and have seen them and their contemporaries re-edit great dance tracks from before they were born, I realise more and more the value in vintage and how "looking back to look forward" is a progressive way of making sure that great music, fashion, design and culture never dies, stays available for future generations and is re-evaluated like all great things should be.

Timeless design deserves an airing for every new generation. Robin Day's classic chairs, Lucienne Day's amazing fabrics, the sharp manly cut of a '60s 3-button-mod-suit, quiffs, Oxford bags and diaphanous dresses, they are all as vital now as the day they were designed. Vive La Vintage!

The Artisan Dandies

Louis XIV was a total trendsetter. The French King laid the foundations for haute couture fashion and a thriving luxury goods market, whilst sporting a wild mane of curls, elaborate frock coats and red-heeled shoes – yet, he still seems a curious and intriguing choice of inspiration for two UK-based women.

Mairon and Toby's love for regal attire, which they mix up with contemporary touches, has spawned their own fashion business creating bespoke historical garments, many of which are crafted by hand as they would have been during the 17th century.

Mairon and Toby photographed at Somerset House, London

Name: **Mairon**
Age: **29**
Occupation: **Freelance Costume Maker**
Lives: **Surrey, UK**

How would you describe your style?

My style is a mix of 17th- and18th-century menswear, Japanese ouji, and Gothic. It is hard to describe it fully since I'm following no rules, and I'm a magpie, so if it glitters, I'll probably add it to my outfit. That is usually how contemporary items find their way into what I put together. There's a lot of brocade fabric, metallic colours and jewellery.

Which historical period has a personal connection?

The court of Louis XIV at Versailles influences this outfit, especially the coat. I adore the clothing from this era because it is the epitome of decadence. The materials are the finest and most expensive and the embroidery is exquisite. I like over-the-top, embellished styles and this era is the best for that – in clothing, architecture and interior design. The court and imperial politics of the time also fascinate me.

When did you start dressing this way?

I've been building up a wardrobe for a few years now. It has definitely been a gradual transformation since this style is not cheap and quick to accumulate the items for. The style has also become more extreme and refined as I've grown in confidence and received more influences. I think the interest in this type of clothing has always been buried somewhere but I was either too concerned with work and studying, or not confident enough to pull it off. As soon as I became confident in myself, the style bloomed.

Where do you get your style inspiration?

I look at a lot of museum pictures of frock coats, cloaks, embroidery, shoes, stockings, and waistcoats, mainly from the 17th and 18th centuries. I used to live within walking distance of the Victoria & Albert Museum, so that was a frequent visit. My friends inspire me too, especially those that are into the Lolita and Gothic styles. I'm lucky to have a lot of connections in alternative modelling and fashion, which is a constant pool of inspiration. I also look around markets, vintage shops and costume sales for inspiration. Camden Market and the people there have been inspirational too.

How do you make your clothing?

I do most of my own patterning, or adapt patterns I find online. A good portion of my fabrics comes

from Goldhawk Road in West London, where I'm recognised as a frequent customer. I also visit fabric shops that supply upholstery and curtain fabric since they lend themselves well to waistcoat and coat making. I adapt charity shop finds and have lately been drawn to buying garments just for their cuffs or a piece of embroidery that I can add to something else. It takes me up to a couple of weeks to make something more advanced like a coat, including the patterning and embellishments. Additional time comes from hand stitching trims, lace or embroidery. I machine sew the basic garments.

Do you dress this way every day?

I dress this way most days, even if I'm just walking the dogs or picking up groceries. It makes me feel good in myself and it's a hobby in itself putting together an outfit for the day. If I'm not feeling so energetic, I will tone the outfit down and it will consist of fewer layers and fewer heavier fabrics. If I'm going into London to meet with friends, I'll go all out with the embroidery, cloaks and sequins.

How long does it take you to put your look together?

Not as long as most would think! I have quite a few faithful items that just lend themselves well to many outfits, so if I'm in a rush, I can put an outfit together in fifteen minutes. Sometimes I like to challenge myself and take a lot longer with hair and make-up. That can take an hour – but I don't think it's much longer than most people take when going out.

Do you have any insights as to why you choose not to dress in the contemporary style?

Contemporary styles change and what I am drawn to does not. I will always like the same types of fabric, good tailoring and embellishment. I'm quite a confident person so it never bothers me that I am seen as 'different' in how I dress.

I have also never felt any desire to follow a trend or style. I feel like a lot of modern styles change very quickly, just so that the shops can sell more products. It is a very throwaway and wasteful culture. In the times that I draw inspiration from, people would keep a coat for their entire lifetime. I really like the idea that some of my clothes are over a hundred years old and still going strong. Perhaps they'll still exist for someone to wear a hundred years after me?

Do you consider yourself to be part of a vintage scene or community?

I feel on the edge of it. I have been to a few events that have a vintage spin to them, such as the Chap Olympiad and the Steampunk Convivial, and have enjoyed my time there meeting people with similar interests. However, I feel that many people in the vintage scene stick to one period or one type of style and are very accurate in its portrayal.

In contrast, I'm all over the place when it comes to time period. My style draws from elements found in this community but fits better amongst the 'alternative' crowd, where you can find a wider range of styles such as punk, Goth or drag. I stand halfway between the two scenes but enjoy both.

How do you mix the historical and contemporary aspects of your outfits?

The most important factor that I like to imitate from historical styles is the general outline. A normal outfit for me will consist of boots or heeled shoes, trousers, shirt, waistcoat, coat and sometimes a cloak or cape. Within this outline I can substitute the historical items of clothing with contemporary ones with a similar shape or feel to them.

I also love the offset of wearing a 17th-century-style coat with modern sunglasses or jeans. Modern fabrics give a much wider range of textures to play with. I have lined a cloak for a costume with the reversible 'mermaid' sequinned fabric that became popular a while back and definitely want to bring it back in an outfit soon! There are also some great faux furs that I want to play with just for the extravagance of them.

Beyond how you dress, what other parts of your life are affected by your interest in period costume?

I have definitely been influenced in the sports I have chosen to pursue in the past. I have competed at archery, fencing and horse riding and still enjoy a good duel when I get the chance!

My partner and I would love to have a carriage and team of horses one day. I also love period dramas and films, even if only to stare at the costumes. My latest fascination has been with the TV show *Versailles*. That is what inspired the coat I'm wearing. We also take our time to visit historical buildings and attend events where there are historical crafts and activities such as jousting.

How did you turn your interest in period fashion into your Dapper and Dust clothing business?

For a while now I have been making costumes on commission for private clients and a few people started to show an interest in the historical items Toby and I had made too. Since we'd made quite a few garments and had the practice and the patterns, we decided to put together our Dapper and Dust website offering our services in this area.

There are a few items, such as cloaks, shirts, lace stocks and trousers that you can buy immediately off the site, since we keep them in stock or they can be made quickly. Other items need to be ordered well in advance as they can take time to pattern and create, and we also offer a bespoke costume making service.

Name: **Toby Curden**
Age: **26**
Occupation: **Freelance Illustrator and part-time Costume Maker**
Lives: **Surrey, UK**

How would you describe your style?

It's a mixture of minimalist modern style and historically inspired menswear.

Which historical period are you recreating and what is the appeal of this era for you personally?

My latest inspiration has been the mid-1600s, and I also make and wear things with late-1700s and Victorian inspiration. One of the outfits that I am wearing here combines modern pieces with a 1600s-inspired coat and a 1700s-style waistcoat.

I've occasionally created pieces with a 20s vibe. For me the appeal is mainly in the craftsmanship and the aesthetics. In the 1600s and 1700s the focus was hugely on rich fabrics, intricate embroidery and structured tailoring, and as a maker the appeal and challenge in that is fantastic. When it comes to more 'modern' looks such as Victorian or early 1900s I have to confess quite a bit of it is for simplicity's sake. You can still find wearable vintage items that you don't feel should be in a museum, and I have a couple of items, like a silk top hat, inherited from relatives that are brought out for special occasions.

What triggered this interest?

I feel like I'm still in the transformation. It's only more recently that my personal style has become

more extreme, though I've been making and wearing costumes for just over four years now. I think the interest in fashion – or perhaps I should call it vintage or alternative fashion – was sparked once I realised you can make your own items as well as find vintage or charity shop treasures, and there is no need to follow mainstream trends or any described style. I never have, really, but beforehand my style was a lot plainer and just picking out decent base items from high street chains.

Mairon has been a huge inspiration in this as well, and seeing them find their 'look' over the years we have known each other has probably influenced me more than anything else.

Where do you get your style inspiration?

Besides museums, it is often from film and TV. Before getting into fashion I cosplayed, which is when you make or buy costumes portraying characters from films, games, books and comics. I was often at events like Comic Con, and it has had a huge boom in recent years, with big international competitions and tournaments going on alongside a large hobby community. Starting to wear some cosplay items day-to-day was my first step into finding my own style.

I would also like to say that while I am very inspired by the aesthetics, I do not wish for society to return to how it was during any of the styles I favour. Modern capitalism and consumerism is not

great, but the colonial oppression and feudalistic systems of the past should only be academic pursuits to learn from to build a better and more equal world.

What is the process of making your garments?

This is a hard one, because it's so very different depending on the garment. So far I have never actually bought a pattern when making something for myself. For a few period pieces I have read authentic pattern descriptions from the time, and then adjusted things to my own tastes. I also tend to look at garments I already own that fit well and trace their shapes.

Fabrics can come from anywhere – online, charity shops, Goldhawk Road in London is a great spot within reach, and in our home town there is a fantastic place selling upholsteries. Furniture fabrics are often brilliant for heavier historical looks.

Most of the time I machine sew what I can get away with, meaning nearly all garments have a combination of hand sewing and machine stitching, with parts that need invisible stitches or extra care being done by hand. When it comes to embellishments it depends on the type. For example, the appliqués on the coat I wore for the shoot are made from many pre-bought appliqués that I then put together by machine, before hand stitching them to the coat.

That garment has so far taken me about three

weeks, but there are still some details to finish off and elements to add. Because the fabric it is made from is so delicate, it was a real challenge and sadly I don't think it will hold up for very long, just because of how thin the outer material is. The waistcoat I wore together with it took me about a month because the embroidery is all done by hand, while I could make the base of a waistcoat like that in a day and a half or so, and a bit longer if doing it all by hand rather than using a machine.

How do you mix historical clothing with the new?

First of all, I love the anachronistic aesthetic. There is something beautiful in the clash of something that belongs somewhere else and putting it together with the here and now, minus the outright time-traveller vibe. I am also a fan of the sleekness of a lot of modern looks, and I love the clash of that with historical opulence.

Secondly, going all-out historical every day would feel like wearing a costume, when you go this far back in time. There is more effort putting it on, it takes longer to get ready, the garments are sometimes more restrictive, and most people you come across ask what play you are part of! Every now and then that is a lot of fun, especially when going to specific events, but day to day it would get a bit much. You still get attention with a 'mixed' style, but usually the comments lean more toward

'cool style' than 'what historical event is going on today and can I take a picture with you?'

Do you dress this way every day?

I kind of wish I did, but I am too lazy! It mainly comes down to convenience. I work from home in my studio and comfort comes before style, so I usually wear jeans and a tailored shirt. I often don't spend much time getting ready if all I am doing is working and perhaps going into the local town to run errands, but if I am heading somewhere else for the day, going into a meeting with clients or to any sort of events I enjoy putting a lot more effort in.

In those cases I'd say it takes me around an hour to pick everything out and get ready, perhaps a little longer. Often I will consider what to wear and make decisions the day before and lay everything out, because I am useless at mornings and not very good at making decisions right after waking up!

Do you have any insights as to why you choose not to dress in the contemporary style?

I think part of it comes from the artist in me, and realising fashion as self-expression and a way to create visual impact is a lot of fun. Then it becomes more enjoyable to apply my own senses of composition and colour matching, rather than getting ready-made ideas from contemporary looks. Through embroidery and making my own garments I also get to employ that maker/designer part that

is always itching to do something new – even if it is inspired by the old.

The trend for fast fashion is also something that doesn't sit right with me, partially from an environmental perspective. Nothing fits anyone quite right, the materials wear out quickly, it's not worthwhile to have things repaired, and the styles change so quickly that your whole wardrobe is out-dated in a year or so.

I was also never a fan of feminine styles and have found that difficult at times. Contemporary menswear in particular bores me, unless you go very high-end or alternative. Through costumes I found a way to be myself that contemporary fashion just didn't mesh with, and then that interest bled into my personal style.

Do you consider yourself to be part of a vintage scene or community?

I still feel very new to it and we have been to a few events, but my style doesn't quite fit into any solid definition, so it's hard to see this blend of styles from older time periods – without going into re-enactment. I have a few friends who are interested in tailoring and clothes making though and I go to things like the Chap Olympiad event.

Beyond how you dress, what other parts of your life are affected by your interest in period costume?

My favourite films and shows are always heavy on the costumes. I sometimes find it difficult to enjoy a modern drama, while I will forgive almost anything in a period drama if there's great clothing!

With my home décor, I don't think it comes into effect much as I am very much for sleek and minimalist styles – perhaps it is the IKEA-bred Swede that I am! But I do absolutely love older architecture, and there again my favourite is the anachronism between the old and the new. And speaking of music, funnily enough there it is again – I much prefer traditional instruments, but mostly I find myself listening to classical covers of modern songs, where contemporary melodies blend with old techniques. Though when it comes to the art and music I consume it is also very varied – my favourite band at the moment is West African Tinariwen.

How did Dapper and Dust come about?

Mairon and I have both been making bespoke costumes on commission for a while now, and people tend to ask about our historical items on a regular basis. Mairon has also worked on designing more garments from scratch, so having an outlet for that in the future and a platform to sell their brand from is a nice thing to set up.

Now we offer bespoke and custom orders on statement fashion pieces, costumes and re-enactment garments. We really want to focus on quality, so we put a lot of effort into finding the right materials and making things well. Another thing that's important is that anyone should have access to the things we make, and we offer adaptations to make these garments available to people who might, for example, have sensory issues or need clothing that fastens in different ways. Since most things are made to measure they can fit anyone and everyone.

The Suburban Lolita

Name: **Yumi Wap**
Age: **28**
Occupation: **Housewife and Mother**
Lives: **Berkshire, UK**

Yumi photographed in London.

Lolita fashion has now become synonymous with Japanese street style, but its roots can be found in the children's clothing from the Victorian period, and the elaborate fashions of the Rococo era. This meshing of European period clothing and Japanese kawaii (cute) fashion has created a very distinctive genre, which has since splintered into three main style subgenres – the Gothic, Sweet or Classic Lolita, all with an underlying romanticism of European history.

Yumi's own passion for Lolita fashion was ignited when she had a eureka moment whilst trying on her wedding dress. Since moving to the UK, the Japanese-born mother has been able to indulge her love for British history through regular visits to historic houses and tea-party meet-ups with other Lolita enthusiasts.

How would you describe your style?

I am a Lolita fashion lover. Lolita is a Japanese street fashion that's influenced by historical European costumes, especially French Rococo and English Victorian children's clothing. My specific style is called classic Lolita. Although there are lots of ribbons and frills, the look is still mature.

Could you tell us a little about your background?

I was born and brought up in Tokyo, Japan. I wasn't a brilliant student, but I always loved music. At the age of seven I joined a choir where I loved singing on stage and wearing frilly dresses like a princess!

I trained to be a musical actress and eventually became a voice actress, but became disappointed with how newcomers are treated in the industry. Not long after I left my agency, I met my English husband in Japan. As soon as we met, we both knew we would marry, despite the language barrier! He proposed to me a few months after we met, and I moved to the UK. I jumped in to this new chapter of my life – just like the first time I was onstage, I wasn't afraid – and this time I wasn't alone, he was next to me, holding my hand.

What is distinctive about the classic Lolita style and how does it differ from other Lolita styles?

There are three main Lolita styles. Sweet Lolita is cute and girly, often with elaborate printed patterns such as cutlery, cakes, sweets and teddies. Skirts are typically worn above the knee or just under, inflated with petticoats or crinolines.

Classic Lolita is more mature and elegant in style. The skirt length is often longer than sweet Lolita and doesn't always require a petticoat. The prints and patterns are often floral or striped.

Gothic Lolita is influenced by Goth fashion. Colours are black or dark and the motifs are crosses, vampires and bats.

What triggered your Lolita fashion interest?

I always adored princess dresses as a child but my parents didn't buy me any frilly clothes, which had probably remained in my heart.

After I moved to the UK six years ago, I was preparing for my wedding and went shopping for my bridal dress. When I tried the wedding dress on I felt elation and such joy that this beauty and quality was surrounding my body! And that was it –

VINTAGE STYLE

I wanted to experience something similar to trying on my bridal dress everyday, so decided to start wearing Lolita fashion. As soon as I had finished the wedding dress fitting, I immediately started to search for Lolita styles online.

Where do you get your style inspiration?
Historical and theatrical costumes, plus vintage from the 50s and the Gunne Sax label from the 70s.

Where do you buy your clothing and accessories?
I mostly buy them from Japan, but I will also buy Lolita-style historical costumes and vintage items from markets and shops in the UK.

Do you dress in this way everyday?
No but I wish I could! I wear Lolita outfits once or twice a week maximum, as I am just an ordinary mother living in the suburbs! But I always wear skirts, generally with lace or bows attached. I don't own any trousers.

#IAMWOMEN

How long does it take for you to put your look together?

An hour and half, maximum.

Do you have any insights as to why you choose not to dress in the contemporary style?

It just doesn't attract me and when I dress up, I always end up looking a bit Lolita anyway. Sometimes this is a problem, because I don't have ordinary formal clothes to pretend to be a normal lady!

Beyond your wardrobe, are there any other aspects of your life affected by your interest in vintage?

I attend vintage and historical events, and of course Lolita tea parties. I love antiques, collecting beautiful vintage tea sets and my master bedroom is decorated in the French Rococo style.

How can people find out more about the Lolita scene?

The English Lolita community organise tea parties and meet-ups through Facebook. London also has Japanese culture events such as the Japan Matsuri in Trafalgar Square every September and Hyper Japan twice a year. There are always Lolitas there that you could try to chat to – I'm sure they wouldn't mind giving you some tips!

The Bricoleur

Name: Stuart Bowden
Age: 40
Occupation: Dance-trained,
now a Performer/Events
Manager
Lives: Manchester, UK

For Manchester dancer Stuart, there's a strong
symbiotic relationship between his appearance and
the spaces he inhabits. He divides his time between
his home in Manchester, filled with vintage relics,
and a stunning Tudor National Trust house in urban
London, where his partner works. There's a real
freedom to his style, which extends far beyond
period enactment, referencing the past whilst
staying very much grounded in the here and now.

Stuart photographed at Sutton House, London.

How would you describe your style?

It's urban, vintage, androgynous and playful. Being a queer black male, I enjoy the exploration of the identities within me. I like that I can be really masculine some days, and quite androgynous or female on other days. I am not a conformist when it comes to style, so I struggle when it comes to events like weddings – what I'm wearing now is a wedding outfit and I might add bondage chaps and harnesses. It's fitting in, but with a twist so I can still identify as me, as opposed to having to wear something formal because it's expected. I like looking like I've stepped out of a different time zone, but bringing it into the modern.

How did you first get into vintage and historical clothing?

I'd always gone to charity shops with my nana and flea markets with my mum. As a child I was fascinated by the little girl in The NeverEnding Story film, and I'd place my mum's necklaces on my head because I didn't see the logic in putting them around my neck. I still enjoy looking at different ways to wear jewellery.

I'd say my vintage voyage really started when I was trying to decorate my council flat and I wanted nothing from Ikea. My neighbour, from whom I inherited one of the coats that I am modelling today, was in her 80s but her flat was hyper-modern. She came to see my flat and said you'd have thought that we lived in each other's houses! She then started to borrow my fur coats and brooches for funerals, because she wanted to look like Liz Taylor.

Do you dress this way on a daily basis?

Strangely enough, it's two-tone now. When I was younger I prided myself on always being dressed up nicely, but now I'm a bit more mature I don't have the time for that daily – I have bills to pay, gardens to garden and a mum to look after! I am quite balanced now and embrace the days when I

can look ragamuffin, not wear any make-up and enjoy a more laidback approach to fashion.

I am lucky that my partner lives in London and when I come to visit I can explore a dual personality and be more creative with my aesthetic. We go to a lot of historic places together and my partner enjoys that I often get looked at as much as the exhibits! I remember being at the Versace Gallery for a show about the Eastern Bloc military artwork and I was wearing a military coat decorated with vintage diamonds. I was looking at a painting

of a 6 or 7-foot black guy who had a similar coat on and people were taking photos of me looking at the picture, mirroring him.

I sometimes look like a moving installation and I play about with that – it's like a performance. I like style as an extension of playing, which I think you should never grow out of.

Aside from charity shops, where do you source your clothing?

I don't really do online as I like to feel, see, try on

and smell things first. I like the journey of acquiring them, just as much as I like owning vintage.

Your style doesn't faithfully recreate a certain period, but incorporates modern elements into historical dress. Can you explain more?

I wouldn't want to look head-to-toe 1950s, as I don't think that's adding anything new, so my look is more a fusion. I like playing about with the modern elements I can introduce. I am a working-class, urban dancer from Manchester, born in 1979, so I've seen quite a lot and to take just one certain genre of style would take away the flavour for me.

Any advice for how to breathe new energy into vintage clothing?

Don't be gender or age restricted. A lot of my clothing is female. I have vintage hats with feathers and veils, from old grannies, which fit my head perfectly as it's smaller.

I also like the external/internal twang to style. For example, I'm wearing a harness outside my shirt rather than inside, and suspenders on my pants as opposed to under. There's sensuality in the restriction, corseting and structure of some garments. I like to start my look with looking at my silhouette and thinking how can I play around with this today? It's about silhouette play.

The Painted Lady

Name: **Natasha (Tashi) Bizarra**
Age: **40**
Occupation: **Full-time mum to my amazing son with Asperger's and 40s clothes hoarder**
Lives: **Ramsgate, UK**

Tashi's look references the pioneering tattooed ladies of the early 20th century, who infringed Victorian gender norms by showcasing their inked skin to fascinated audiences at circuses and sideshows. Earning far more than their male colleagues, these artfully adorned women fell from sight with the advent of television and the decline of travelling circuses.

In recent years tattoos have transitioned from outsider into mainstream culture, yet Tashi still manages to align her style with a bygone era through the old-school symbols and references that grace her skin.

Tashi photographed at Vintage by the Sea Festival, Morecambe.

How would you describe your style?

American and British 40s wartime fashion, with a dash of tattooed lady thrown in.

Do you dress this way every day?

Most weekends we do vintage and 1940s events around the country, as my partner is a performer and I wear original clothing to all of these events. My everyday wear is a mix of original 40s and some repro.

Are environmental concerns a factor in wearing vintage?

Absolutely. I reuse, repair and recycle all of my clothing. In the wartime era, they had to make-do-and-mend and I try to follow this. I love bringing tired and wounded items back to life.

Where do you get your style inspiration?

Much of my inspiration comes from 1940s America. The tattoos I have are also inspired by designs from that era. I just love the history involved with the old American sideshows, with the tattooed ladies such as Artoria Gibbons and Betty Broadbent. To me they symbolise the individuality of their eras. I also get a lot of inspiration from my beautiful friends around the world, who I attend 1940s events with. I love music of all genres but particularly the dancing and music of the 1930s and 40s, so much of my inspiration comes from there as well.

Where do you source your clothing and accessories?

I visit charity shops, thrift shops and use social media groups. A lot of my clothing I now source from America, as I'm currently more drawn to the styles and colours of that era.

Beyond the dress, which other aspects of your life are affected by your interest in vintage?

Everything! It's my lifestyle – I attend events, dances and my whole social life revolves around events of the era. My partner dresses in original clothing and my 15-year-old son also wears vintage, even to school.

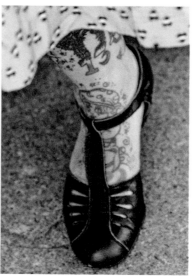

The Up-Cycling Queen

Name: **Mei Hui Liu**
Age: **43**
Occupation: **Artist, Fashion Designer and Curator**
Lives: **London, UK**

East London designer Mei Hui Liu was one of the early pioneers of up-cycled fashion. Armed with a second-hand sewing machine and some salvaged textiles, she started up her Victim fashion label in the late 90s, opening up a boutique just off buzzy Brick Lane.

More recently, she's opened Victim Fashion Street – a gallery space adorned with antique furnishings and clothing, where people are invited to come and play dress-up, whilst enjoying a very English tea party.

How would you describe your style?

One of a kind vintage and up-cycled textiles. The Victorian era, punk and Lolita princesses influence me. I love mixing a vintage nightdress or wedding dress with contemporary accessories and headpieces.

Do you dress this way every day?

Yes I do. In the olden days I used to dress up to go to nightclubs or parties, but I don't do that anymore so now I just dress like this in the day to meet friends for tea.

Photographed at Mei Hui's Victim Fashion Street Gallery,

When and how did you become interested in vintage style?

I really became interested in vintage style when I moved to London in 1994. Before that, I was obsessed with designer brands such as Dolce & Gabbana, Romeo Gigli and Vivienne Westwood. Then one day I just decided to sell all my designer clothing at Portobello Market and start again, this time just wearing vintage and up-cycled clothing. This led to me starting my fashion label, Victim, in 1999.

Are environmental concerns a factor in wearing vintage?

When I started it I didn't really know about sustainable or ethical fashion. It was purely about my passion for vintage textiles, particularly Victorian lace. But over the years I found that my label was always in the ethical section at fashion exhibitions, and because of the current environmental issues, it helps me to keep my passion alive. What I do is not about making the perfect dress or following trends – it is about helping people to be unique.

Where do you get your style inspiration?

I grew up in Taiwan listening to English music from the 80s and I was really into the New Romantic style. I have since lived in Italy, Paris and London and this travelling has helped me create my own vision and style.

Could you describe how your fashion gallery space works?

After 20 years of running my fashion label, I had the idea of opening up a sustainable fashion gallery on Columbia Road in East London. It is an installation space where people can come to have the experience of dressing up in the clothing, sample the delicious food sourced locally from the East London area, and have a traditional English tea party. It is an inclusive space where adults, children and all genders can have the experience of dressing up and have their photo taken.

What do people enjoy about visiting the gallery space?

People can enjoy the experience of dressing up without having to feel like they need to own the clothing, and it means that I can share my wardrobe and vision, rather than my clothing being hidden away in a wardrobe. This concept of borrowing clothing for tea parties and photo opportunities is one that can travel to different galleries or spaces, and means I can share my passion for food, fashion and art with others.

How does the fashion gallery differ to how you've decorated your home?

My home is very simple, so it's white, modern and contemporary. My gallery on the other hand is a riot of antique and vintage, which makes it the perfect reflection of my personality!

Any tips for how to breathe new life into vintage clothing?

I have always said that you shouldn't give up on your used clothing – fix it, up-cycle it and bring it alive again! Every item can be precious and can one day become vintage, so buy clothing that you really like and wear it over and over again.

The Wartime Darling

Name: **Hattie Bee**
Age: **21**
Occupation: **Vintage Singer and Screenwriting Student**
Lives: **Yorkshire, UK**

Since she was a young girl, Hattie dreamt of being a singer. Rather than listening to pop, her early musical education was imitating singers such as Nat King Cole, feeding her aspiration to be like one of the late, great stars of the bygone era.

The Lancashire singer and student can now be found entertaining with wartime favourites at vintage events across the UK, wearing her trademark austerity-chic styles from the 30s and 40s.

This was fashion at its most frugal, and there was little creative leeway as WW2 regulations required that nothing went out of fashion before it wore out. The amount of fabric used, length of skirt, pockets and unnecessary decoration were all heavily controlled. However, fashion still managed to flourish during the era, with a boom in functional utility wear, and a resourceful attitude to mending and reimagining existing clothing.

How would you describe your style?

My style harks back to the golden age, the 1930s and the 1940s; a time when cuts were more sleek and elegant, and the fashions were pretty.

Do you dress this way everyday?

I do. I will go into university in a 1940s dress or skirt, with my hair pin-curled and make-up always done immaculately. It's safe to say that the rest of my course mates think I'm mad!

Are environmental concerns a factor in wearing vintage?

I would say so. We live in a world of throwaway fashion, and when you consider these dresses that I wear, they're 80 years old and have been cared for so well. During the Wars you couldn't get hold of new clothes as readily as you can now, so you had to make-do-and-mend, ensuring you got the most out of an outfit.

Where do you get your style inspiration?

I love reading informative books about the fashions of that era. I also like looking on Google at pictures from the era.

Where do you source your clothing and accessories?

Absolutely everywhere. People give me their unwanted clothes, there's eBay, charity shops and vintage fairs. You just have to have a very keen eye.

Beyond the dress, which other aspects of your life are affected by your interest in vintage?

Vintage influences so much of my life. My house is decorated in a 1940s style, although I do also have my mod cons. It also influences my university work. As a writer, I write a lot of period dramas because my knowledge of the 40s is so rich, there's always something to write about.

Hattie photographed at Vintage by the Sea Festival, Morecambe.

London's Lone Star Cowgirl

Outlaw, singer and Western aficionado, Sarah Vista cuts a unique figure on the grey streets of North London. Her punchy murder ballad songs, embroidered Western shirts and suede chaps stem from her childhood love for Spaghetti Western films.

Having found acclaim in recent years as the gun-toting Sarah Vista character, she has since realised the dream of performing at Sergio Leone's original stage set in Spain, and has become a cover-star of *Rock and Roll* magazine.

Name:
Sarah Vista
Age: **Less!**
Occupation:
Cowgirl
Lives:
London, UK

How would you describe your style?

Sarah Vista is a fugitive, strong-willed cowgirl hell bent on retribution, so my style reflects this character. I guess I have a somewhat masculine look inspired by the outlaws of the Old West and some of the Hollywood stars of the silver screen and music worlds combined.

When did you start dressing this way? Was it a gradual transformation?

In my fantasy I've been a cowgirl since I was a toddler. I used to dress up in old rags and re-enact movie scenes as a child, so I've always liked dressing up and exploring different roles as a kind of escapism. I collected bits and pieces over the years, but honed my look and made my final transformation in 2016 when I released my first work.

What triggered this interest and what is it about Western wear, and in particular the clothing worn in Spaghetti Westerns, that appeals?

I've been interested in cowboys, cowgirls and all things related since I was a small child. I used to watch the old movies on my rocking horse when I was a toddler, and think I was in the movie with the gang, one of my earliest and happiest memories. I think the clothing worn is largely practical for riding the range and being ready for action in a gunfight! I find this hugely appealing, it's strong, fearless and determined and a fantasy I enjoy being immersed in. I mix this up with classic cowboy wear like chaps, gun belts and a replica of the poncho Sergio Leone put Clint Eastwood in for the *Man With No Name* character he portrayed in Leone's epic trilogy of Italian movies from the genre affectionately dubbed 'Spaghetti Westerns'. This is where the grittier, more comedic influence on the look comes in!

Where do you buy your clothing and accessories? Is it all original vintage or do you also wear reproduction?

I have a mixture of original pieces including items from the 1800s, the 40s, 50s, 60s and modern current pieces by designers who design repro items in a similar style. I've got a series of custom outfits I've been having made to fit my character as it's developed.

Is the clothing and image an important part of your whole performance? What is your favourite outfit for performing?

My clothing is integral to my character. I sing and perform as a no-holds-barred retribution-wreaking

wild woman of the West, so I need my clothing to reflect this. I have a few pieces I wear constantly as I feel strong in them, including a pair of vintage boots with white steer-heads on and an old vintage suede fringed skirt that's so comfortable, I could live in it.

I always wear (vintage and modern) cowboy hats but have a favourite fawn-coloured one that suits me best. I ritually dust my boots in actual dust from the Sergio Leone film locations I frequent before I go on stage.

Who are your style icons?

My childhood style icon was Doris Day in *Calamity Jane*; I subsequently fell in love with Joan Crawford as Vienna in *Johnny Guitar*. Clint Eastwood and Eli Wallach from the Leone movies are definitely strong iconic references for me. I like the classic Hollywood cowboy look seen on the likes of Gary Cooper and Kirk Douglas. For a more modern daily look I adore the ultimate Hollywood icon dressed down in classic denim: Marilyn in *The Misfits*.

Do you dress this way every day?

Yes. At the absolute least I always wear something with Western influence, even if it's a modern Western shirt, necktie or repro 1950s denim. It gives me confidence.

Do you have any insights as to why you choose to dress in this style?

I love to re-use and recycle. I never ever buy new leather, suede or animal products, as I'm an avid animal lover. I don't believe in the disposable high street, low quality, quick turnover culture. It's terrible for the planet, badly made and lacking in every way. Modern stars and fashions don't excite me at all.

Do you consider yourself to be part of a vintage scene or community?

Since I found my feet as Sarah Vista, I've pretty much forged my own little scene and am a big part of that. I do have some wonderful, lovely vintage aficionados who come to my club and shows and I consider them great friends. I've also been embraced by the alternative music and film worlds.

Growing up I felt unconfident and a bit of an outsider. Since early childhood I struggled to fit in with scenes and groups and the type of people attracted to them, so it's incredible that the character I created and live in has changed my life so much, in such a positive way. I've created my own bubble that I'm happy living in and now I see myself less of a loner, more a lone-star!

Do you have any recommendations for people who are also interested in Westerns?

Definitely watch any 50s and 60s Westerns you can get your hands on. I'd recommend David Miller's *Lonely Are the Brave*, Nicholas Ray's *Johnny Guitar* and most anything by John Ford. There's something gloriously intriguing to be found in most vintage movies when looking back at a time and style. As

for the more modern Italian westerns of the 60s – everything by Sergio Leone is amazing. I would also recommend the *Great Silence* and *Django* by Sergio Corbucci.

As for travelling, the US is amazing for Western movie and culture lovers! My spiritual journey through the sacred Navajo land, home to Monument Valley, was life changing. I'd definitely recommend going if you ever get the chance! No photographs or words will ever do this majestic land, nor its people justice.

Almeria in southern Spain is home to one of the most breath-taking mountain ranges in the world and some of the most incredible locations, which is why so many Westerns were shot there. Head to 'Mini Hollywood' in Tabernas to see the Western town designed by Carlo Simi for Sergio Leone, and 'Western Leone', the location for Claudia Cardinale's Sweetwater home in *Once Upon a Time in the West*. It's a movie lover's paradise.

Finding Lost Angeles

Rachel and Nate live in a glamorous Art Deco building, on a palm-tree-lined Los Angeles boulevard. Walking over the threshold into their apartment is like lavishly travelling back in time. A modern television set is perhaps the only clue that we are in the 21st century. Aside from this, the entire space is a carefully curated homage to Rachel and Nate's passion – The Golden Era of Hollywood.

Rachel and Nate photographed at home, Los Angeles.

The history-loving couple recently moved to LA and started their blog, Finding Lost Angeles, which is dedicated to preserving the city's storied past – the pieces of its history that are long gone, and those that remain today. At the weekends they can be found painstakingly researching and exploring the city's nostalgic attractions, from Frank Lloyd Wright's Hollyhock House to the Western Costume Company – who dressed many of Hollywood's starlets during its Golden Era, from the 1920s to the late 1950s.

This period is considered Hollywood's most spectacular, with the advent of sound, big stories and even bigger budgets, and a stable of alluring actors that included Marlon Brando, Cary Grant, Rita Hayworth, Lauren Bacall and of course Marilyn Monroe. Academy-Award-winning costume designers such as Edith Head made their mark on the era by celebrating the female form with sensual silk evening gowns, nipped-in waists and elegant, voluminous skirts. Charismatic leading men such as Humphrey Bogart and Cary Grant offered up sharp-suited templates of masculinity.

It is the interplay between movie costumes and the fashion world that was particularly evident during this time – from the fashion house Givenchy collaborating with the actress Audrey Hepburn to create onscreen magic, to 'cinema boutiques' opening up in department stores so

that women could purchase silver screen replicas.

Both Rachel and Nate radiate that old-world glamour that their chosen era has become synonymous with. Their love for the period was ignited by the movies of the era but now manifests itself in the almost forensic attention to detail that they pay their dress and interiors. In an enchanting apartment in Los Angeles, the Golden Era of Hollywood truly lives on.

Name: **Rachel Kafka**
Age: **29**
Occupation: **Recruiter for the entertainment industry**
Lives: **LA, USA**

How would you describe your look?

Styles from the 1940s and 50s that are classic, glamorous and feminine.

What is it about the golden era of Hollywood that appeals?

The clothing was tailored to women's bodies in a way that you can't find today. My interest also comes from living in LA and experiencing the architecture and the exciting vibe of the city.

It's more than just the clothing then, and more of a lifestyle choice?

Absolutely, the clothing came later but I've always loved old music and antiques. When I was a little girl, about three or four years old, I would watch old Hollywood movies with my grandmother. I always gravitated towards older time periods. The clothing side was gradual and I started collecting about ten years ago.

Do you dress this way every day?

No, but I wish I did! I work in a corporate office, so my look still has a 40s flavour but is much more subdued. In the evenings and the weekends, I am full-on vintage!

How long does it take to get ready?

An hour on average. I sleep in curlers the night before, so it's just the make-up which takes 20 minutes, then brushing out my hair.

Where do you get your style inspiration?

I always come back to the starlets from the 30s, 40s, and 50s. I love Rita Hayworth's style and her poise, plus Marlene Dietrich, Betty Grable, Marilyn Monroe. I am also active on Instagram where there is a big vintage community that I draw inspiration from.

Where do you buy your clothing and furniture?

It's been years of collecting. Nate and I have been together for nine years, piecing things together from flea markets, thrift shops, Craigslist and antique stores. For clothing I sometimes shop on Etsy. My favourite stores in LA are Play Clothes, Paper Moon and Rag Moth. I have a larger shoe size so can never seem to find vintage shoes, so I buy repro shoes.

Why do you not dress in a contemporary style?

Even from a young age, I have been someone who likes to dress up a lot and be noticed. There's something special and a bit sentimental about earlier eras, especially living in a city like LA where it's all around you, it's easy to feel an attachment to that. I feel like the clothing is an expression of these interests that have always been a part of me. That's why the clothing came later, because it's more than just an aesthetic to me.

Would you like to have lived in the era?

I would love to time-travel for a few days, but I am actually very happy living in the 21st century! I do think it's easy to over simplify or romanticise many of the hardships that people went through – with the war and civil rights struggles.

Do you consider yourself to be part of a vintage community?

Social media has made vintage style much more accessible. Our blog comes from me being a history nerd and wanting to preserve the history of LA. We are still quite new to the city so are starting to meet people here, and there are definitely pockets of people who are interested in the same period of style. We have also been to the Viva Las Vegas vintage meet up.

Beyond the dress, which other aspects of your life are affected by your vintage passion?

Music-wise I listen to Ella Fitzgerald, Etta James, The Boswell Sisters and the Andrews Sisters. For film, the movie that started it all was *Gypsy* with Natalie Wood, who had this sexy, classic look, which has quietly inspired my style interest over the years.

Name: **Nathan (Nate) Hennigan**
Age: **29**
Occupation: **Attorney**
Lives: **LA, USA**

How would you describe your style?
My look is an eclectic mix and match. I rarely wear head-to-toe vintage. I wear a contemporary look with a vintage accent, such as bow tie or a loud vintage print shirt.

How did your style evolve?
I came to it later than Rachel and our interest has grown together. When I was growing up I listened to classic rock and slowly my tastes have changed. I started listening to more country, rockabilly and blues from the 40s and 50s.

What interests you about this era?
There was so much growth and optimism at that time, particularly in LA. You could hop on a bus from Iowa and be a movie star! It had this classic, glamorous feel but also with a seedy underbelly, which you see in vintage noir films or books. There's a great mix of intertwined cultures and opportunities that came together at the same time.

Where do you buy your vintage?
I pick pieces up at vintage stores around LA or there's a place in Orange County called Joy Ride that's really great. As fun as it can be to browse online, it feels a bit like cheating. I enjoy the hunt, and being able to try things on and see how they fit. When you find that one piece – the style, fit and the price are right – there's a satisfaction to that which you can't find elsewhere!

As an attorney, how much creative freedom do you have in your work wear?
In the professional space that I work in, there isn't much. But I can still subtly bring vintage elements in, such as high-waisted pants as part of a suit that I would wear in court.

Why are you not choosing to dress in a contemporary style?

Vintage offers a fit and quality that contemporary clothing doesn't. It might have been around for 50 years, but it will be around for another 50 years as it's so well made, often by hand. In comparison, a mass-produced shirt might fall apart in a few months.

Tell us a little more about your blog Finding Lost Angeles

It came about as a way for us to document what we were doing on the weekends, finding gems in the city that were off the tourist trail – we kept thinking 'Wow, I can't believe people don't know about this place!' Our next project is to publish a book.

When we were writing about The Brown Derby we came across this book called *Hollywood Cocktails*, published in the early 30s, before prohibition ended. These cocktails reference Hollywood stars or restaurants around at the time. Our plan is to recreate it with a new foreword. It would be cool to preserve this slice of Hollywood history.

The Star-Spangled Restaurateur

Texas Joe has become something of a legend on both sides of the Atlantic. Originally hailing from The Lone Star State, he moved over to the UK and caused a stir when he appeared on the business-pitching show Dragons' Den, dressed head-to-toe in a rhinestone-encrusted Western suit, topped off with a ten-gallon hat.

He's since launched a successful range of beef jerky products and opened London's most authentic southern BBQ joint, whilst maintaining an impressive collection of Western vintage tailoring, including items by tailoring legend Nudie Cohn, who kitted out Elvis, Gram Parsons and Roy Rogers.

Name:
Joe David Walters
Age: **46**
Occupation:
Restaurateur
Lives: **London, UK**

How would you describe your style?

A hybrid of Texas and Hollywood. It's a flashy, fantasy cowboy look – not a cowboy who worked the range, but a cowboy who worked the backlot.

When did you start dressing this way? Is it a style you saw around you growing up in Texas?

Growing up in Texas I was more into alternative rock. I wasn't really into country style as it was everywhere. I grew up in a small town called Portland in Texas and the cowboys were real-life farmers. It was when I left and moved to Austin that I started wearing the boots, because my dad always wore the boots and hat. Then I moved to LA and suddenly I missed the look and music of Texas, so I started dressing more like the kids that I grew up with.

What is it about vintage Western wear that appeals to you personally?

They are one-of-a-kind pieces, which I consider to be like fine art. My biggest nightmare is walking into a place and I'm wearing the same thing as someone else! With a Nudie suit it has the date that it was made and who it was made for, and you know that it was an important moment in that person's life.

I collect these things knowing that one day they should be in a museum. They were generally made for an entertainer or performer, who would have been very conscious of their personal style.

For me, vintage is about the craftsmanship and the history. They created this look years ago and it's still relevant to modern style. If you look at the last few years of runway shows from Calvin Klein and Gucci, to Prada, they've all done a Western-wear look, but none as good as the original – Nudie!

I remember seeing the episode of Dragons' Den when you walked out of the lift and your outfit caused such a stir. As well as having a great product, you clearly understood how to use your image to get noticed. How important do you feel your clothing has been to your career?

It's a key part of my identity. In retail, you try to get a unique selling point. My USP is that I look like a Hollywood creation. If you're wearing a suit like that, people will instantly ask 'who's that dude?!' because you have a completely different vibe, particularly wearing it in England, but even in Texas or LA as people just don't dress like this any more.

When I was selected to go on Dragons' Den, I knew I'd wear that suit and I didn't tell the producers until five minutes before I went out there, as I knew it would have that effect. When I walked in, the dragons were confused, which was a strong weapon.

Joe photographed at his Texas Joe's restaurant, London.

Could you tell us a little about the gold Nudie/Elvis jacket and how you came to own it?

It was in the possession of a Hollywood stylist. In joints like Western Costume in LA, there was a whole rack of embroidered Nudie suits that stylists could pull from. In the 80s, when they didn't know what it was, stylists would go and borrow this stuff and if they didn't return it they would just get charged $100. So a lot of stuff disappeared!

A stylist had this jacket and put it up for auction with Heritage Auctions. There's a picture of the actor Hugh Laurie wearing it in GQ and it was originally made for Harry Nelson. Nudie said it was made from the same bolt of fabric as the famous gold jacket that he made for Elvis, so it's like the cousin of Elvis' lamé jacket.

Where do you buy your clothing and accessories?

I started buying in the 90s, pre-internet and living in LA, where I'd just find things in thrift shops. Then eBay came along and things got a whole lot more accessible. Before that, a lot of this stuff was with private collectors and traders – it was this mysterious world that you weren't allowed into. Still, a lot of the best stuff is celebrity and musician owned and if you don't have a connection into that world, you'll never see it as it's just being moved around in these higher echelons than I operate in.

I also pick things up at traditional auction houses. Any Hollywood memorabilia auction will typically have one or two Nudie, Turk or Rodeo Ben pieces, and quite often they slip through the cracks so you can get them for a decent deal. I typically pay less for a really great vintage piece than you would pay

for a new designer piece, or perhaps even an off-the-rack piece. For $150 you can buy a plain Nudie shirt, moving into $300–400 for an embroidered one, and between $500–700 for a full suit. It's not astronomical and if you compare the prices to what people paid for them originally, it's a bargain!

Do you dress this way every day?

I don't wear vintage every single day, as the pieces are too unique and special. I wear repro denim and know a guy in Japan who reproduces Wrangler 50s jeans, or Levi's vintage collection, which I team with a Western shirt, and always a cowboy hat.

Could you tell us about your involvement with the clothing label Union Western Clothing?

I met Jerry Lee Atwood, who is a chain stitch artist and tailor, a few years ago. I know a lot of touring musicians as I used to be in a band and have a venue in Los Angeles, so I started telling people we were making these Nudie-style suits; high-end couture Western-wear, with chain stitch embroidery that was probably the best around.

We were trying to keep alive the art of one-off pieces, which make your dreams into reality, incorporating themes and motifs that mean something to you into the clothing.

We started out by effectively making suits for free or at cost, for musicians that we knew would be in the public eye, knowing that would raise the profile of the brand. And it worked! Jerry currently has a two-year waiting list for a suit. Now artists like Post Malone, who is this chart-topping rapper who had the biggest selling debut album of all time, we've made him about five suits. It's interesting to see it come out of country music, and move into rap and hip hop.

If someone were interested in getting into the vintage Western scene, where would you recommend they start out?

Books like *How the West was Worn* are great for seeing a piece and researching designer's name, then trying to pick up a piece on eBay, which is a great tool.

The Vintage Mama

Name: **Annette Kellow**
Age: **35**
Occupation: **Writer**
Lives: **London, UK**

Annette is a London-based writer, occasional vintage model and quite possibly West London's most glamorous parent. Her look is ultra classic and wearable, with a wardrobe filled with 50s-style day dresses, teamed with vintage furs and a head of perfect pin curls.

She can often be found foraging for vintage finds at Portobello Market – the Golborne Road end, naturally, where the vintage insiders know there are still bargains to be found.

How would you describe your style?
Vintage with a focus on the 50s.

Do you dress this way every day?
Mostly, with the occasional day off!

What is it about the mid-century that interests you?
I love how clothes were made to measure and made to last. They paid a lot more attention to detail and took care of their clothes. I also love how clothes in the mid-century were feminine and flattering, accentuating and beautiful. It was like tailor-made clothes were the norm back then!

Is it just the clothing or are other aspects of your life affected by your interest in vintage?
I like their attitudes – people seemed to be polite and concise in their everyday dealings. I like that the pace was slower in terms of sending letters and telegrams and fate played more of a part. Now

people just look at someone's insta-story to find out where they are! I also really enjoy the music, furniture, and aesthetics of the 50s.

Where do you get your style inspiration?
I have quite a lot of old books and love reading biographies – one of my favourites is about Sophia Loren.

Where do you source your clothing and accessories?
I look online and am part of a few groups that sell at a discounted price. I like Portobello Market, but the trick is to haggle as they always mark the prices up. But my all-time favourite is car boot sales, and not in London! I go to the countryside where my parents live and I always get amazing bargains. Once I got an almost new 1950s dress for 75p. Then the man proceeded to open the back of his van and said, 'You like that old stuff? There's plenty more in here.' I died and went to heaven!

Annette and Felix photographed at home, London.

Are environmental concerns a factor in wearing vintage?

I think vintage is sustainable and if made well can be used for longer than more modern clothes. But I do think people get worried about wearing fur, even if it is a family heirloom. I read an article recently that buying new faux fur is very damaging to the environment, and although I personally would never wear new real fur, I don't mind vintage.

Name:
Elaine Stott
Age: **44**
Occupation:
**Fitness
Instructor and
Specialist
Exercise
Instructor**
Lives:
Rochdale, UK

The Hitchcock Heroine

Elaine's distinctive style is a nod to the female actors in Alfred Hitchcock's influential films. The Hitchcock heroines as they were known, which included Grace Kelly and Tippi Hedren, were immortalised on the big screen by costumier Edith Head, wearing twin-sets with nipped-in waists, full ballerina shirts or dramatic couture evening gowns.

The Hitchcock look relied heavily on Dior's New Look, a style introduced in 1947, with vast skirts, tight bodices and wasp-waists. The revolutionary look came under fire for its extravagant use of yards of fabric, considered unpatriotic in the shadow of post-war austerity. The dramatic New Look silhouette, teamed with Hitchcock's cinematic mastery, created a femme fatale icon that contemporary fashion houses continue to revisit.

How would you describe your style?

I put together a mixture of repro and original 1950s clothing, with some 1940s thrown in.

Do you dress this way everyday?

Unfortunately I can't as my work outfits tend to have to be Lycra! However, in my non-work time I'm always vintage styled.

Are environmental concerns a factor in wearing vintage?

I do like the fact my clothes are mostly vintage, therefore there are no extra pressures anywhere in the world to make them.

Where do you get your style inspiration?

Firstly it was my nana – a stunning, perfectly put together lady! I also find inspiration in the fabulous movies of the 1940s and 1950s and those wonderfully glamorous actresses of Old Hollywood. And now, Dita Von Teese, Pinterest for old images of the 40s and 50s and rockabilly style models.

Where do you source your clothing and accessories?

It's mainly online. I love Etsy and have several favourite sellers on there. As I'm also getting better known on the vintage scene, I now have several traders who know my style and size, and will message me if they have something come in that

Elaine photographed at Vintage by the Sea Festival, Morecambe

they think I'd be interested in.

I have items made my a friend who has a company that specialises in making clothes to original vintage patterns – so I can order my own colour, fabric and have items made exactly to my measurements, which I love! I also attend vintage fairs, events and find all sorts of pieces there.

Beyond the dress, which other aspects of your life are affected by your interest in vintage?

Oh everything! My home is vintage focused and I have an original English Rose 1950s kitchen, a Tiki-style conservatory, a gentleman's country club living room and a mahogany antique-themed boudoir bedroom. We also own a classic car and a cute little campervan.

My love for vintage has also helped with my work, as some of my clients are older adults who love all my stories and seeing my outfits. I lecture four times a year on vintage at the local Townswomen's Guild. I try to work vintage into everything I can!

The Modern-Day Pin-Up

Name: **Lady Eccentrik**
Age: **28**
Occupation: **CEO of Entertainment Soul Limited**
Lives: **London, UK**

Lady Eccentrik's style is rooted in the classic pin-up looks of the 40s and 50s. The image of the high-glamour pin-up women took off during WW2, when posters of Betty Grable lined the locker doors of G.I.s, and kitschy paintings of the Vargas girls became a hit for *Esquire* magazine.

Lady Eccentrik's own style combines the glamour of the mid-century pin-up with her Jamaican heritage and desire to always look dapper. Her background in the performing arts is evident in the pure theatre of her image.

What vintage era are you interested in and why?

The 1940s and 1950s, because of way the clothing shapes the body. When I am dressed in this way I can walk with my head held high.

How do you bring your Jamaican heritage into your style?

Jamaican people take a lot of pride in how they dress and are always well coordinated – especially the males! No matter our economic status, fashion comes first. It's part of Jamaican culture that you could never look at us and determine our financial or social status from our dress.

Is there a vintage scene in Jamaica?

Absolutely not! In Jamaica, vintage would be called 'old bruk' and people just don't want to be seen in someone's second-hand clothing.

In Jamaica, fashion and music go hand in hand. If you say vintage to someone in Jamaica, they think of the 70s, 80s and 90s and the clothing is affiliated with the music, in particular to the dancehall scene.

When did you start dressing this way?

I started to dress like this four years ago, but I've always wanted to be different to my peers. When I was 11, I discovered Grace Jones and started mixing 70s and 80s clothing into my wardrobe. I lived in Manchester at that time and there wasn't much access to original vintage fashion, so I would make my own pieces.

Then I discovered the performer Dita Von Teese, and I realised this is a good look for ageing gracefully. I have a ten-year plan and a vision of how I see myself looking, but I am not quite there yet. I am a work in progress!

Where do you get your style inspiration?

Pinterest – I have mood boards for everything! I also like researching vintage clothing patterns and watching old movies. I love the costume designer Edith Head, so will watch films she has worked on just to see the costumes. My shirt/skirt look is inspired by a design she did where the dress tapered in at the ankle.

Lady Eccentrik photographed at home, London

How hands-on are you with making your clothing?

When I first became interested in vintage style, I was really excited about it and basically threw away everything I owned and started again – I wouldn't advise this! Since then I have learnt to sew and get inspiration from vintage patterns, so I can be more creative.

Where do you buy your clothing and accessories?

Mostly from eBay but reproduction clothing brands also sponsor me, in return for reviews.

Does working in the creative industries allow you more freedom to express yourself in your work wear?

I can't dress as feminine as I would like, as the music industry is male dominated, so I have to have that edge in my fashion at work. When I am on the road on tour, I will wear a t-shirt with the artist's branding on, paired with a vintage circle skirt and vintage accessories.

How long does it take you to put your look together?

I get dressed in my mind the night before, so it's

actually quite quick! My make-up takes 45 minutes and my hair doesn't take long as it's a wig. I am proud of my natural hair and have recently been doing vintage-inspired natural hair videos, as I have been getting interest from black girls who are interested in vintage style but don't want to damage their hair with straighteners. But for my own personal look, I like to wear a wig.

Do you have any insights as to why you choose not to dress in the contemporary style?

When I came to the UK from Jamaica at the age of 11, a whole new world opened up to me. Although I am quite introverted, I also wanted to stand out and express myself with my clothing. When I am dressed in this way, people want to come over and interact. I like to make the world a bit more colourful!

The Vibrant Thrifters

Hannah's style is a riot of colours and textures, like a meeting between Carmen Miranda and Frida Kahlo. For Hannah, going vintage is much more than just wearing a certain style of clothing – it's part of a broader make-do-and-mend philosophy which ties in with current concerns regarding plastic waste and consumption.

Hannah and Sean photographed at Vintage by the Sea Festival, Morecambe.

Name: **Hannah O'Kelly**
Age: **44**
Occupation: **I paint, draw, sew, bake, needle felt and make weird and wonderful creations**
Lives: **Gloucestershire, UK**

How would you describe your style?
1930s to early-1950s vintage

Do you dress this way everyday?
Yes, it's a mix of original, repro, and homemade

Are environmental concerns a factor in wearing vintage?
Our initial drive came from the aesthetic of vintage style and the quality of timeless style and durability. The minimal waste and make-do-and-mend ethos of the 40s has always appealed. More recently we have been moving towards being single use plastic-free, and this aligns with the ethos of the way we live. I strongly disagree with and disapprove of cheap throwaway fashion.

Where do you get your style inspiration?
I grew up with old movies, watching Fred & Ginger. In the 1980s we witnessed a lot of influences from the 30s and 40s, for example in the way bands styled themselves and in movies such as *Blade Runner*. I now find inspiration from original vintage pictures shared on social media and from the events we attend.

Where do you source your clothing and accessories?
From local vintage shops in Stroud – where we're friends with the owners – or from stalls, vintage shows we go to, occasionally online from selling groups, and I also make some of my clothes. I do buy reproduction clothes online, as these are easier to buy online once you know your size.

Beyond the dress, which other aspects of your life are affected by your interest in vintage?
The less wasteful ethos of vintage appeals – of valuing what you have and making use of it. I like the fact that the things we own have a history, and they can tell you about the time that they came from. People in the vintage scene tend not to throw things out, instead they get passed onto new owners who will continue to value, maintain and repair them.

Name: **Sean O'Kelly**
Age: **45**
Occupation: **Admin Manager**
Lives: **Gloucestershire, UK**

How would you describe your style?

I mainly dress in clothes in the style of the 30s through to the 50s, but I am slowly drifting back to teens and 20s. Although this period includes periods of wartime austerity in Europe, I prefer to look towards Hollywood and America for inspiration, as many would have at the time.

Do you dress this way everyday?

Yes, even if I am being casual it would be Hickory Stripe Dungarees or 1939 US Navy pattern jeans, a 30s-style polo shirt and leather boots. The last modern clothes that I brought were tracksuit trosuers, to go to the physio in.

Are environmental concerns a factor in wearing vintage?

Initially not, although I was never a fast fashion kind of person. The enviromental concerns have become a bonus, as they are now part of everyday life.

Where do you get your style inspiration?

Old photographs are a great inspiration. The best are photos with everyday people in, rather than fashion photographs. Also looking through the racks of vintage clothing dealers is a great way to understand what colours and styles people wore. Keep an eye out for the details.

Where do you source your clothing and accessories?

Due to my size, a lot of my clothes are reproduction. There are a few good suppliers for men. Although modern men's tailoring is very different to that of the 30s to 50s, there have been numerous revivals of previous styles over the decades since, so charity shops are also a good bet. The jacket I am wearing in the photo was purchased from an online gentleman's outfitters, overall it has the look of the 30s, but the lapels are a little smaller. Accessories such as ties, tie clips and cufflinks are generally original and come from vintage dealers, car boots and charity shops. Also, I don't mind wearing dead people's clothes.

Beyond the dress, which other aspects of your life are affected by your interest in vintage?

We attend numerous vintage festivals, weekenders and events all over the country; to such an extent we have not had a foreign holiday for years. Luckily we have found a vintage festival in Italy so we can combine the two next year. We once had a spare room for guests, but it is now full of our wardrobes!

Name: **Lindsay Jarvis**
Age: **35**
Occupation: **Senior Editor,**
Atomic Ranch **Magazine**
Lives: **Palm Springs, USA**

Palm Springs is a mecca for lovers of mid-century design – from the tracts of perfectly preserved modernist housing, to the vintage interiors and wardrobes of its inhabitants – Palm Springs is a desert town seeped in glorious Technicolor nostalgia. The city initially had its heyday during the Golden Era of Hollywood, when it became a playground for movie stars, after the studios decided they wanted their artists within a two-hour radius of the set at all times. In recent years it's received an influx of young, design-savvy newcomers, who have come to soak up Palm Springs' good weather, good design and good times.

The mid-century aesthetic permeates Lindsay's life, from her stylish modernist house in a resort-style complex overlooked by the dramatic San Jacinto Mountains, to her vintage interiors, wardrobe and even her job at a leading Modernist design magazine – all aspects have been touched by her passion for the past.

Do you think there's a link between living in Palm Springs and your personal style?

I was drawn to Palm Springs because of the mid-century vibe. The architecture, the lifestyle, and the preservation efforts are all geared towards the mid-century and appreciation for the aesthetics of that time period. I've certainly had to adapt my personal style to the hot desert summers though! 1940s beach-style is one of my all-time favourites and I think that look pairs perfectly with Palm Springs.

Could you tell us a little about how you became senior editor of Atomic Ranch *magazine and how this work influences your style?*

I was a freelance writer for *Atomic Ranch* magazine for about two years. They would assign me a home tour and I would interview the homeowners, architect, or interior designer. I took on the Senior Editor position early January 2019.

My personal style has not really changed or been influenced by my work at *Atomic Ranch* since I've been dressing this way for about 14 years now. However, it does seem to be a nice fit for the *Atomic Ranch* brand since the architecture focuses on the mid-century.

Lindsay photographed at home, Palm Springs.

How would you describe the way you dress?

Everyday elegance. Casual, comfortable and functional vintage. I really love styles from the 1920s to the 1960s, but I find the pieces that work best for my body and lifestyle are usually from the late 1930s to the early 1960s. While I really love the extravagant gowns and fancy dress of those eras, I tend to gravitate towards wearable styles that are actually functional. Cool and sturdy fabrics that are comfortable and stand up to everyday wear and tear.

Do you dress this way everyday?

I do! Some days certainly end up looking more 'vintage' than others, but this is the way I dress all the time. My hair has a frizzy and fine texture, so I use either foam rollers or pin curls to set it. It's the only method I've found that works for my hair! Heat styling does not work for me.

Are environmental concerns a factor in wearing vintage?

Absolutely! Not just for clothing, but also for home décor. It helps to cut back on materials/sourcing for new products, but also on all of the extraneous packaging and plastic used to transport larger items like home goods. If you can re-use an item, why not?!

Where do you source your clothing?

I love to go to physical shops when looking for clothing and accessories. It's such a great way to connect – not only with the item – but also with other vintage enthusiasts. There's a lot of great shopping in Southern California. Lately, I've also been buying directly from other vintage enthusiasts on Instagram.

Sewing and knitting are two of my favourite hobbies, so I do make some of my own clothing

VINTAGE STYLE

using vintage patterns. I also have some reproduction pieces, especially shoes. I have issues with my feet, so I only have a few pairs of true vintage shoes. Remix Vintage is a fantastic reproduction company with comfortable and beautiful options. I also love Loco Lindo for their breezy and beautiful rayon crepe pieces.

Beyond dress, which other aspects of your life are affected by your interest in vintage?

I'd like to point out that I love the aesthetics of the mid-century, but not the values. Vintage fashion, not vintage values! It's purely about the looks for me... but I'm also interested in mid-century homes. We are currently fixing up a 1964 condo with some fun vintage pieces!

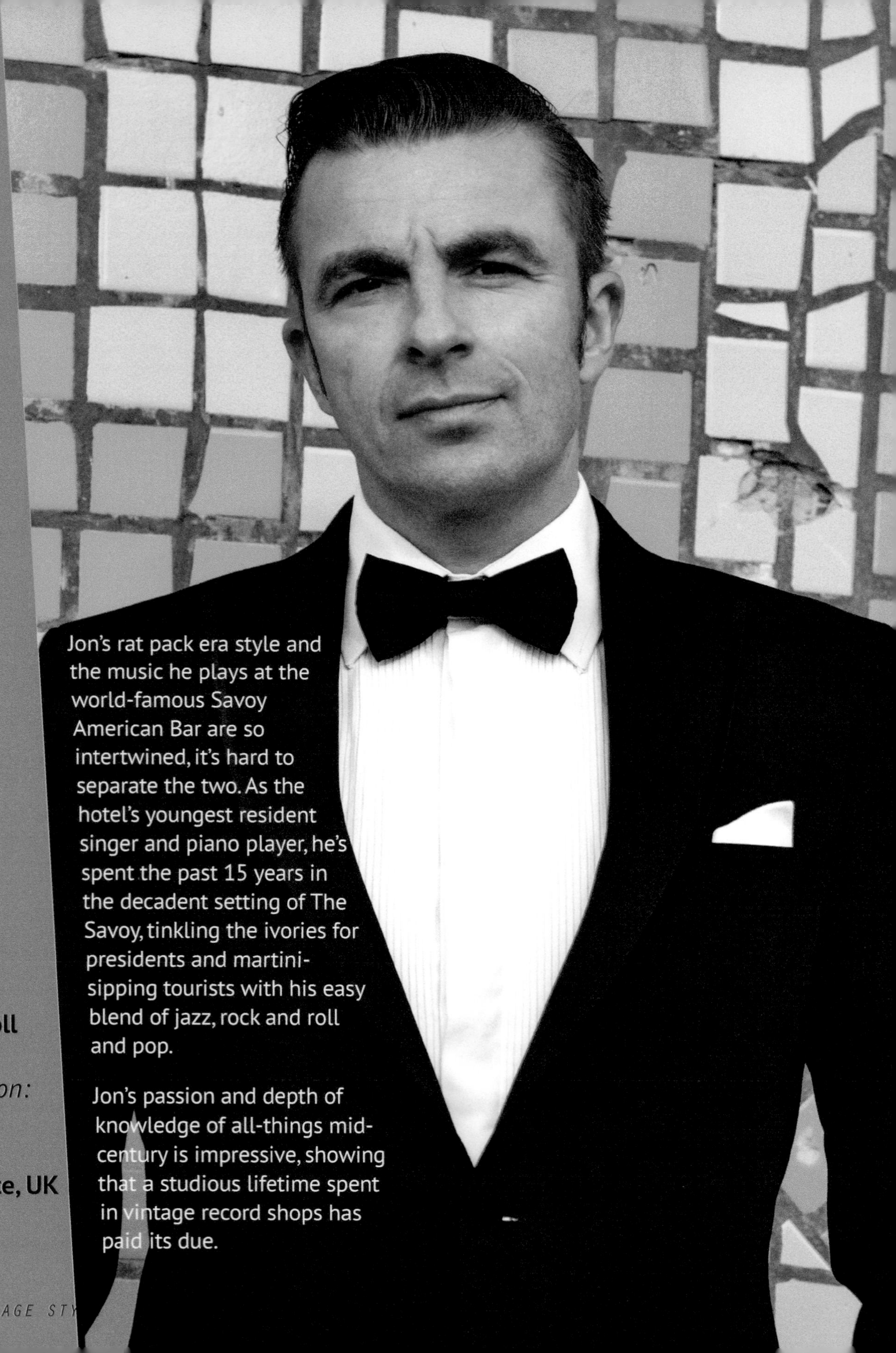

Jon's rat pack era style and the music he plays at the world-famous Savoy American Bar are so intertwined, it's hard to separate the two. As the hotel's youngest resident singer and piano player, he's spent the past 15 years in the decadent setting of The Savoy, tinkling the ivories for presidents and martini-sipping tourists with his easy blend of jazz, rock and roll and pop.

Jon's passion and depth of knowledge of all-things mid-century is impressive, showing that a studious lifetime spent in vintage record shops has paid its due.

Name:
Jon Nickoll
Age: **41**
Occupation:
Musician
Lives:
Ramsgate, UK

How would you describe your style?

1950s/1960s vibe. If in doubt wear a blazer and pop a pocket square in it!

Which bygone era interests you most and why?

I love the US and UK 1950s and 1960s styles. I think the pride and attention men gave to grooming in the mid-20th century really found its groove, and so many contemporary styles and trends seem to hail from this time frame.

The crossover between music and style seems to be important in your look. How has your musical interest impacted your wardrobe? Were there any pivotal moments when you discovered an artist who then impacted your style for example?

I'm always fascinated by what the famous of this era wore when they weren't working. British stars like Billy Fury, and American ones like the Everly Brothers, The Beach Boys, Dean Martin and of course Mr Presley; these icons looked jaw-dropping cool 24/7, and often their own personal wardrobes are hipper than the things the publicity studios dressed them in.

I'm a huge Elvis fan, and I think the way he was styling himself from pre-fame right 'til his final days on earth, is a lesson to anyone who gives a hoot about such things.

My Elvis baptism occurred when I was about seven years old. The 1970 MGM documentary *That's The Way It Is* was on TV, and as the camera followed Elvis during rehearsals and preparations for the upcoming season in Las Vegas, I was spellbound by not only the humour and humility of the man, but especially the achingly cool way he dressed. Patent leather boots, pinstriped slacks, high-collared shirts, the custom shades – it all blew my mind.

Growing up in a middle class household in Margate in the 1980s, I'd never seen anything remotely like it. I quickly became known as 'Elvis' at school, a nickname I had no problem with whatsoever. I used to drive my poor mother insane, badgering her to make me capes and oversized belts, so I could stride around the streets of Margate karate chopping and performing to imaginary audiences!

You've been the resident singer and piano player at The Savoy hotel in London for 15 years. How would you describe the iconic hotel and its ambience?

Clearly the hotel is one of the most famous in the world, and yet The Savoy has the unique ability to operate on many different levels, bespoke to whoever is experiencing it.

My HQ The American Bar is a perfect example of

this. To mixologists, the bar is simply sacred turf, and not an evening goes by without 10 or 15 wide-eyed cocktail types entering the bar to experience the place they've no doubt read about for years. On the other hand, there could be a couple having a quick G&T before catching a post-work dinner, who enjoy the environment, but may not necessarily be genned up on the history of the room. Also, there are the solo business travellers, who enjoy a cocktail, catch up on work emails, enjoy the atmosphere, and watch the world swirl by.

The American Bar, like the hotel itself, creates a magical stage for all these folks to play on as they choose. I feel that The Savoy never has to shout to get attention; it's earned its fame!

The Savoy is known for its old-world charm. Would you say your personal style has adapted to the hotel over the years, or were you originally attracted to playing there because of its vintage heritage?

To me this is the most extraordinary thing about these last 15 years in the hotel, at the risk of sounding clichéd, is that The Savoy has led me on a cultural, musical, philosophical journey.

A week before my opening night, my agent Gary Parkes reminded me that I would need to get a tuxedo for the gig. This was out of my comfort zone, as at 23 I had never sported evening dress. He accompanied me to Savoy Taylors Guild – right next to the Savoy – and subbed me my first Savoy pay cheque in order to get the suit!

I quickly learned the importance of linking my musical style with the clothes I was performing in, something that had never crossed my mind before. The little rituals of putting on the cufflinks, giving the shoes a quick shine and checking the bow tie in the mirror, all get me into the appropriate mind-set to play.

Beyond the actual gig, the hotel and the people in it have had a big impact on my style peccadilloes. I greatly admired the way many of the Savoy bartenders dressed when they weren't working. I clocked it, and gradually found myself doing similar – jeans are fine, but smarten up the look with a jacket, fitted shirt and boots. Now I'm

sailing into my early 40s, I really feel what I wear matches where I'm at.

How do you dress from day to day?

I have loads of blazers, some vintage, some new, but always with a vintage nod. Add a white pocket square, and match with whatever the weather dictates, a nice well-fitted shirt or wool jumper. I have never been a fan of wearing trainers unless I'm forcing myself to exercise, so on my feet you'll

find either black or brown suede shoes, or black leather Chelsea boots.

Where do you source your clothing and grooming products?

Through my record and book buying addictions, I have developed a bit of an eBay and charity shop fetish and can happily spend 30 minutes or so typing in 'Jacket 36 REG' and flicking through never-ending images of potential wardrobe additions on eBay!

Similarly, I love a good rummage through a charity shop, which are often great for vintage cufflinks, 50-year-old woollen ties, and occasionally – if the gods are smiling down on you – a suit! I do get the core basics from more straightforward outlets, such as the Levi's store in Covent Garden.

I must add that I also have a kink for sourcing classic colognes and hair products – all these elements help build up your spiritual armour and let you go into battle feeling fully dapper and hip. Some of this stuff is super easy to come by; Elvis wore 'Brut', 'Hai Karate' and 'Jovan' fragrances, which are all still in production, and therefore on my bathroom shelf as we speak.

My wife isn't a huge fan of overpowering cologne and there was a traumatic and as yet unsolved mystery of my very expensive bottle of Knize Ten (James Dean's scent of choice) being mysteriously removed from my cabinet. Fear not reader, I'm bidding on a replacement on eBay right now! For hair pomade I use Royal Crown, which is hard to find in a physical store but pretty straightforward online.

What are your top three albums of all time?

An outrageous question, and of course the answer will be different every 5 minutes, but as of today, right now, I'll go for:

1. *Sea Shells*, Peggy Lee
2. *Elvis Is Back*, Elvis Presley
3. *What's Going On*, Marvin Gaye

You've travelled the world with your music. Are there any destinations or festivals that you'd recommend for vintage fans?

I do travel a fair bit as a musician, and I always think travel is a great opportunity to let your freak flag fly and really pimp out the vintage look. I have a couple of super-cool 1960s suitcases (charity shop finds again) which are just the right size for hand luggage, so bringing these beauties out always puts a spring in my step when in transit. I was lucky enough to play on the Orient Express last year, and I really felt like I was in a movie.

I'd always recommend popping into junk stores and antique places when in unusual locations too. What we deem as treasure, other countries may call trash. I've found some awesome Elvis records when in funky little back street flea markets in Hong Kong.

Have you any tips on how to breathe new life into a vintage style?

I strive to take elements from or attempt to create the overall effect of a period look. Just yesterday, I saw a great picture of Marvin Gaye on the back of a CD booklet, wearing a light grey suit with a yellow buttoned down collar shirt. Seconds later I was on eBay seeking out a yellow shirt! I think follow and hunt down the things that make you go 'oh yes'. It really doesn't have to be an expensive pursuit – just have a wish list and the universe will reward you for your organisational skills.

The Memphis Rock and Rollers

Nina

Tiffany

Nina and Tiffany have the most rock and roll workplace in America – Sun Studio in Memphis. The legendary music studio is the birthplace of rock and roll music, giving us not only the first rock and roll single back in 1951 with the release of *Rocket 88*, but also launching the careers of Carl Perkins, Jerry Lee Lewis, Johnny Cash and The Memphis Flash himself, Mr Elvis Presley. There's something about the gritty history and musical heritage of the city that works its way into the Memphis look – a devil-may-care attitude mixed with a respect for the past.

When not working at the Sun Studio hit factory, Nina can be found listening to vintage vinyl, and musician Tiffany brings her unique blend of classic love ballads, jazz, R&B and old country standards to venues across Memphis.

Name: **Nina Kathleen Jones**
Age: **25**
Occupation: **Operations Manager/ Public Relations for Sun Studio**
Lives: **Memphis, USA**

How would you describe your personal style?

It's always evolving! It's a touch of vintage with a modern execution. I never leave the house without a nice, strong cat eye. I really like colour blocking/monochromatic; right now I have black hair and generally wear all black clothing. Before the black, I had pink hair and would wear varied shades of pink with a bold pink lipstick.

Do you feel working at Sun influences your style?

Oh for sure! I went through a phase of diving deep into the vintage rockabilly style. Everyday was victory rolls and petticoats. Since then, I have toned it down but vintage 50s style still inspires my dress. Sun has guests daily from every corner of the world – we get to see every nation's fashion represented and we get the chance to recreate that in our own way. Who says you can't wear stripes and polka dots in the same outfit?!

Do you think there's a Memphis style?

Just like Memphis music, Memphis style is hard to put into one category. 'Grit' might be the best term to describe it. Memphians are not overly concerned with what anyone else thinks of them. Who cares – just wear what makes you happy!

Where do you get your clothing?

I absolutely love being able to purchase second hand clothes. It feels nice to be able to give love to something that has been discarded. I do a lot of shopping at local thrift stores and antique stores. And of course, online shopping has been a game changer. Thank God for eBay!

Nina and Tiffany photographed
at Sun Studio, Memphis.

Name: **Tiffany Harmon**
Age: **32**
Occupation: **Tour Guide and Rock
n Roll Storyteller at Sun Studio**
Lives: **Memphis, USA**

How would you describe your personal style?
I would say that I draw inspiration from a lot of
different eras of style. One day I'm wearing a 50s A-
line floral dress with heels, another day Indian
broom skirts and the next day I'll be wearing a ratty
Velvet Underground tee with jeans and cowgirl
boots. It's just all over the place!

*Do you feel working at Sun influences your
style?*
I think that working there definitely gives me a
great reason to dress up when I'm on the clock,
especially dressing for the period. Working at Sun
and having a super-relaxed dress code has given
me the courage to try new things style-wise and to
dress the way I've always wanted to.

How would you describe the Memphis style?
To me, Memphis never seems to follow any fashion
trends. Memphis is about throwing together
random things that make you happy to look at in
the mirror. Memphis is thrifty A.F. and proud of it!

Where do you get your clothing?
Target or Dillards for most of my dresses, or
sometimes Modcloth or Eshakti if I want to spoil
myself. I really don't spend a whole lot of money on
clothes. Although the new Goodwill that just
opened in Midtown seems to have taken all of my
money lately!

The Lone Greaser

Name: **George Loveday**
Age: **18**
Occupation: **Student**
Lives: **Sheffield, UK**

George is a young man out of step with his surroundings. Whilst his peers are into indie rock music from the local Sheffield area, George has set his sights on another era and culture altogether.

The greaser style that George is so passionate about was popularised by American teens in the late 40s. It originated from working-class males who were disillusioned and heavy on attitude, having been excluded from the post-war boom. Rebelling against the era's preppy office wear, the greasers chose slicked-up hair, a leather jacket worn over a white fitted t-shirt, denim jeans and motorcycle boots as their uniform.

The greasers congregated in gangs through motorcycle and hot rod clubs, meeting to soup-up their cars and listen to rock and roll and doo wop. Although youth culture during this era was often villainized, it was the greasers in particular that struck fear into the heart of middle America, seemingly confirming the worst fears about rock and roll's link with teenage delinquency and violence.

The greaser subculture soon hit the big screen with the release of *The Wild One* in 1953, with Marlon Brando's leather-clad character offering a blueprint for aspiring greasers. James Dean followed hot on his heels, as the slick pompadoured outlaw in *Rebel Without a Cause*. Greasers have continued to crop up on the big screen, with *West Side Story* in the 60s and the musical *Grease* in the 70s.

Perhaps because of their gang culture roots, the Greasers were always an edgy style tribe. However, their legacy look – the pomp, leather jacket and denim jeans – continues to symbolise youthful rebellion and the aesthetic lives on today as a quintessential part of 1950s Americana nostalgia.

Tell us about your style.

I have been dressing as a 1950s greaser for about two years. My inspiration comes from the music and icons like James Dean.

How did you become interested in the greaser style?

None of my friends or family dressed this way when I was growing up. I remember when I was younger being in the family car and Elvis came on the radio. I instantly fell in love with his music, so looked him up and thought he looked really cool! Through Elvis, I then found James Dean and Dean Martin and just thought, 'Wow, this is for me'.

Do you see a distinction between rockabilly and greasers?

Yes, greasers were classed as the hoodlums of the 50s and were into motorbikes and hot rods. It's very specific to America. Rockabilly is safer and has a wider mainstream audience than greasers – it's more Gene Vincent and leopard print.

What is it about the Greaser era that appeals?

Greasers are often outsiders; they're the ones who weren't popular at school. I also don't fit into today's society because of the way I dress, but my friends accept me. I feel that it doesn't really matter what you're into, as long as you're a nice person.

Given the choice, would you like to have lived during that period?

For the music, fashion and the cars, yes I would love to live in this era. But because of issues such as segregation in 50s America, I absolutely wouldn't. 50s Britain and 50s America were two completely different things.

Where do you source your clothing?

Apart from Levi's jeans and a few shirts, my entire wardrobe is true vintage. Original 50s stuff is really rare but when you find it, it's usually in good condition, as it was well made using quality fabrics. I go around vintage shops in Sheffield or when I'm visiting different cities. I don't use the Internet as 50s sizes were very different, so you really need to try things on.

Where do you get your style inspiration?

I like Elvis and James Dean but I also like the classic look of Dean Martin, Eddie Cochran, Roy Orbison and Frank Sinatra. These people have really influenced our fashion now – James Dean was one of the first people to make denim mainstream and he really pulled it off.

Describe your favourite outfit.

It's Levi's 501 jeans with turn-ups, paired with either a t-shirt or polo shirt. I also wear Levi's 751 jeans, as they're baggy and fit perfectly over a boot. Teaming jeans and boots is an important greaser look. I will also wear vintage trousers and shirts, but it's hard to properly relax in them.

How long does it take to get ready?

About 1 hour and 15 minutes, including a shower. Most of this time is spent on my hair, which takes 15 minutes to blow dry, then another 10 to add the grease and comb through. I put on my outfit before doing my hair, as pulling a t-shirt over my hair would ruin it.

What products do you use?

I use old-style pomades like Black & White, Dax, Royal Crown, and Murray. Greasers don't use hairspray, as putting it over the oil leaves white flakes in your hair. Greasers' hair never sets, that's why we carry combs in our back pockets.

Do you ever dress in a modern way?

No, I always have a hint of 50s. If I go out on the town, I might have to tone my look down a bit so I'll wear Levi's and casual 50s-style shoes like Converse or PF Flyers.

Do you have any insights as to why you choose not to dress in the contemporary style?

My style really reflects the 50s and 60s rock and roll music that I'm into. If I dressed like my friends

in a modern way – in the slim-fit jeans with the trainers – I would feel like a pretender.

Are you part of a vintage scene or community?

I don't see rockabillies or greasers on the streets around me, as they're all down in the South of England. So I started my Instagram page because I wanted to find people who share my interest. Social media has meant I have connected with greasers all over the world

Is it just online or do you have face-to-face meet ups?

I am part of Chesterfield rock and roll club and we have all day events where people bring their Cadillacs and play rock and roll into the early hours. It's a really good atmosphere and like being in a time machine, transported back into another era.

What other aspects of your life are influenced by your greaser passion?

I can only decorate part of my bedroom in the 50s style, as I share it with my 20-year-old brother, who is not into the greaser scene at all! But I do watch television from the era – *The Dean Martin Show* is really funny – and I collect things like cigarette tins from the 50s and 60s. I love the history of these things. That someone would have carried that actual tin in their pocket over 50 years ago – to me that history is much more valuable than something contemporary and manufactured.

Will you always dress in this style?

Yes. Some people just like the style and don't listen to the music, so for them it's just a passing phase. But I'm so into the whole greaser scene – the music, films, cars and fashion, that I think I'll live it forever.

Rockin' in Sicily

Name: **Sayaka Alessandra**
Age: **32**
Occupation: **English Teacher, Blogger and Elvis Tribute Artist**
Lives: **Trapani, Sicily**

Sayaka is a 50s-loving rockabilly blogger and Elvis tribute artist, living in a Sicilian coastal town. She is passionate about the rockabilly scene, which originally sprung out of Southern America in the early 50s, blending country and blues to create this fledgling form of rock and roll.

Rockabilly hit the mainstream through artists such as Carl Perkins, Wanda Jackson, Buddy Holly and of course Elvis Presley. Although it was a fairly short-lived genre, having fallen out of favour by the early 60s, its influence had a ripple effect which continues to be felt today – from the music of bands like the Kings of Leon and The White Stripes, to the style of celebrities such as Gwen Stefani and Paloma Faith.

Style-wise, mid-century rockabilly men favoured button-down two-tone shirts, cuffed pants and denim jeans, sports coats, bold prints and a healthy dose of bubble-gum pink. For rockabilly women, at the safer end of the fashion scale there were full skirts and petticoats, teamed with twin-sets, pumps and ponytails. Think Sandra Dee in *Grease* before her metamorphosis. The racier rockabilly styles owed more to pin-up models of the era and veered towards figure-hugging pencil skirts, Jayne Mansfield-style tight sweaters and stiletto shoes.

Although the 60s were quiet on the rockabilly front, from the 70s onwards rockabilly has continued to ride the waves of revival. Major rockabilly conventions such as the annual Viva Las Vegas, attract thousands of stylish enthusiasts who faithfully recreate the mid-century lifestyle and look. Rockabilly has also splintered into subcultures such as psychobilly, which mixes 50s rockabilly with British 70s punk, or teetered on the caricature with Japan's Yoyogi Park rockabillies, with their exaggerated, gravity-defying quiffs.

Although rockabilly remains fairly mainstream, it is still a little unusual to find one of Europe's leading rockabilly voices living in a small, traditional town on the island of Sicily. Whilst Sayaka might stand out from the tribe locally, online she has found a loyal fan-base who follow her for the latest updates on all things Elvis, rockabilly clothing, retro food, and anything kawaii, inspired by her duel Italian-Japanese heritage.

How would you describe your style?

1950s rockabilly, nostalgic and Elvis inspired.

What is it about the American mid-century era that appeals?

Basically everything! The music was real, the fashion was classy and I love the food. My idea of fun is to visit a diner for a burger and milkshake, followed by cherry pie or a banana split for dessert, whilst listening to Elvis on a jukebox. I may be Japanese-Italian, but my soul is from Memphis, Tennessee!

How did your musical career start?

It started in 2008, when I started uploading videos of myself singing covers of my favourite oldies. Then the following year, my cover of Elvis' *Baby Let's Play House* was featured on YouTube's homepage during Elvis Week. I still remember my friend in The States contacting me to say, 'Sayaka, you're on YouTube's front page!' It was incredible!

My video got half a million views and the subscribers worldwide skyrocketed. From then on, I officially became an Elvis Tribute Artist. As Buddy Holly once said, 'Without Elvis, none of us could have made it'.

When did you start dressing this way?

I've been attracted to the fifties since I was a little girl but I couldn't really find any retro stores in Italy. Then in 2012, I discovered online shops selling vintage apparel, as well as a few authentic vintage shops in Rome.

I also found a tailor who would make vintage reproduction clothing for me, by copying pictures that I liked of 50s models and celebrities. From then on, my wardrobe started to represent my personality – the outside finally matched the inside. My colleagues would tell me that I now looked like 'la ragazza di Elvis' – Elvis' girlfriend!

Where do you get your style inspiration and source your clothing?

I get my inspiration from Elvis, movies like *Grease* and TV shows like *Happy Days*. I get my clothes from Etsy or eBay and I sometimes find retro-inspired clothes at modern chains like H&M or Zara. Polka dots, stripes and gingham never go out of fashion!

Do you have any insights as to why you choose not to dress in the contemporary style?

I'm a nostalgic person, so contemporary style doesn't really represent me. There are days when I'm lazy and dress modern, but I'm happiest and more in tune with myself when I wear something that is vintage style.

I think this is because of the songs I sing and the music I've always listened to – I was brought up on Elvis records thanks to my mother. I feel like I belong to another generation.

Do you consider yourself to be part of a vintage scene or community?

There's no vintage scene where I live, so I'm the only person who dresses like this. People actually stop me on the street to ask, 'Why do you dress like this?' 'How do you do your hair?' or 'Are you part of a musical?' It is via the web that I feel that I am part of a vintage scene, or when I go to 1950s-inspired events in the north of Italy or abroad.

Do you always dress like this?

No, I don't dress up like a pin-up model to go to the supermarket! If I'm performing, being photographed or going out for dinner, then I'll complete my 50s look with heels and more make-up, but for everyday I go for a more toned-down vintage look. I'll wear my beloved red Keds sneakers, teamed with polka dots, gingham or stripes. I'll always have a flower or red bandana on my head, often with an Elvis-inspired vintage roll with my hair, red lipstick and winged eyeliner. Last but not least, cat eye sunglasses are a must!

The New-Wave Rock and Roller

Name: **Sally Walmsley**
Age: **22**
Occupation: **Recruitment Consultant – it pays the bills**
Lives: **Morecambe, UK**

The neo-rockabilly style has been around since the 90s, mixing references from the original mid-century trailblazers with styles from contemporary indie bands.

Since rock and rollers burst onto the scene in the 50s, music and fashion have had a reciprocal relationship. It's hard to imagine a young Elvis performing on stage without his trademark quiff and upturned collars, the Ramones minus the leather jackets, or Prince without the purple attire and heeled boots. The image and the music go hand in hand, both feeding off each other.

How would you describe your style?

Indie rockabilly

Do you dress this way everyday?

Yes I dress this way as much as I can and will add a bit of flair to office-wear at work.

Are environmental concerns a factor in wearing vintage?

Not so much a concern but a social awareness. I try and buy from charity shops and vintage kilo sales as much as I can to reduce waste but sizes don't always permit, as vintage clothes are usually so petite and dainty. I always try to get sustainable footwear that I can get resoled, rather than throw away.

Where do you get your style inspiration?

Films, postcards, social media, seeing others at vintage shows, scooter rallies and TV series.

Where do you source your clothing and accessories?

eBay, vintage kilo sales, retro shops, Manchester's Northern Quarter and charity shops.

Beyond the dress, which other aspects of your life are affected by your interest in vintage?

I mainly listen to northern soul and indie pop music. My friendships and relationships usually share a common interest in all things vintage and retro.

The Mod-Son

Name: **Bill John Roth**
Age: **15**
Occupation: **Student**
Lives: **East Sussex, UK**

At just 15 years old Bill is one of the few mod teenagers on the scene, but his association with the tribe runs through his veins. Much of Bill's wardrobe originates from his father's own mod period and Bill also grew up near Brighton – a seaside town long associated with the mod gangs.

The mods originally started out in the 50s as a hip group of London guys who listened to modern jazz, earning them the nickname of mods. Clothing was always an essential part of mod life, with parka jackets, sharp tailoring, fitted polos and Clarks desert boots becoming the gear of choice.

In the 60s the mods caused moral panic when they clashed violently with rival rocker gangs, before the mod style went mainstream to became Carnaby-Street-cool as part of the Swinging London movement. The style was revived in the late 70s with the release of the film *Quadrophenia* and mod-influenced bands such as The Jam and The Specials. Bill is part of a new wave of mod-revivalists, who meet up in British seaside towns to share their appreciation for the music, style and scooters of the mod life.

Bill photographed in Brighton.

How would you describe your style?
Smart mod.

When did you start dressing in this way?
I was about seven and my older brother triggered my interest. I wanted to be like him so I started asking my mum to only buy me mod clothes.

Did anyone else in your family dress this way?
My dad dressed as a mod from the ages of 15 to 26, but he stopped when he became a father. He still listened to music when we were younger though, from bands like The Who, The Jam and The Small Faces. But when my older brother and I started dressing like mods, it inspired my dad to start wearing the clothing again, so it's come full circle. My dad's cousins were original mods. They were in Brighton the same weekend that the fights happened.

What appeals about the mod era?
The violence. If the fights were to happen again, I probably would get involved. I also like the fashion and the music, bands like Madness, The Specials and Bad Manners.

What are the key components to a mod outfit?
Rule number one; you've got to look smart. I would either wear a suit jacket and tie, or a polo shirt and

desert boots, although I'm trying to get my hands on some bowling shoes. And of course the parka jacket – I'm never without the parka.

Where do you get your outfits?
Some of my clothing has been passed down from my dad or my brother. One of the family heirlooms is the jumper with Pete Townshend on the front that my dad wore to see The Who in the 70s. There are a few mod shops in Brighton, such as Jump the Gun and Bone, so I'll go to these if I can afford it, or I might buy replicas from the high street.

Who are your style icons?
My dad and my older brother.

Do you dress like this every day?
Not at school as we have a uniform, but I wear my parka over the top of my blazer. I also always leave the bottom button of my suit jacket undone – it's a mod thing. If my teacher has a go about the uniform this year, I don't really care, as it's my last year.

How long does it take to get ready in the morning?
About 15 minutes – I just tell my mum what I want to wear.

Why are you not dressing like your school friends?

I want to be individual. I hang around with a group of rejects at school – one is a punk, one is an emo and another is a Goth. At school people try to find popularity through wearing certain branded clothing, but I'm just not interested in that.

The really smart mods, who are well dressed and might have the best scooters, are known as the face. I am the face of my school, so younger kids might come to me and ask advice about becoming a mod – I always just tell them that it's expensive!

Outside of school, are you involved in the mod community?

Yes, I recently went to the mod festival in Brighton and an older mod came up to me and said, 'it's nice to see the new breed here'. When I go to places like Music Mania I see people in their 20s, but I am usually the youngest mod at these things.

Aside from the clothing, which other aspects of your life are influenced by mod culture?

My bedroom is decorated with *Quadrophenia* posters and I've got a scooter clock on my wall. I aim to get a scooter as soon as I am old enough.

Any advice for people interested in mod culture?

Come down to a scooter run and just start talking to the mods. Start listening to the music, as it's a big part of the scene.

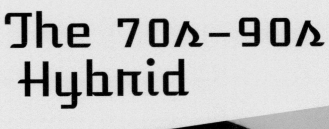

The 70s-90s Hybrid

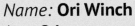

Name: **Ori Winch**
Age: **24**
Occupation: **Nanny by day, Actor by slightly later in the day**
Lives: **London, UK**

When Ori was growing up in Israel, vintage and thrifting were not the norm. As a teenager she managed to carve out her own look by tapping into her mother's wardrobe and masterfully merging her favourite style decades – the 70s and 90s – to create her own distinct aesthetic.

Now living in London, she's often found adding to her vintage collection through thrift shops and kilo sales, mixing it in with family heirlooms.

How would you describe your style?

My friends joke that my aesthetic moves between boho-witch and straight-up-hippie. I feel at home in an all-black, flowing silhouette but also love playing with funky patterns and textures, so I guess they're mostly right! The 70s and 90s are big influences, but other decades and centuries are great inspirations, alongside the people around me.

What is it about the 70s and 90s that appeals to you?

I grew up in the 90s listening to 70s music, and I think that made those decades, specifically, synonymous with familiarity and ease for me. They give me a sense of identity that definitely bled into the way I dress.

Stevie Nicks and Joni Mitchell are huge icons to me, both in music and style, but I am also just as inspired by Rachel's outfits on *Friends* and my mom's photo albums from her 20s.

Where do you source your clothing?

It's a bit of everything, really. Some basics are store-bought, a lot of my clothes and nearly all of my outerwear and accessories are thrifted, and some of my favourite items are hand-me-downs from my mom.

Are environmental concerns a factor in wearing vintage?

Absolutely. I think these days it's very easy, especially as a young person, to fall into the culture of fast fashion and excess. We all do the best we can, and I know I still have a way to go but I am very aware of it. I buy second hand whenever I can and try not to contribute to mindless consumerism for the sake of it. It's definitely a work in progress.

Any advice on how to breathe new life into old clothing?

It sounds obvious, but make it your own. For example, I wear a lot of men's vintage coats that were massive on me when I found them, so I got the shoulders taken in and rolled up the sleeves to make them fit my shape.

Adding accessories and making small alterations here and there can make a thrifted piece look like it was made for you. It's extra helpful to have some basic sewing skills, then you can do it yourself!

Another tip would be to pair a more 'out-there' vintage item with a simple outfit, if you want to ease yourself into styling second-hand pieces. Crazy patterned trousers with a plain tee, a monochrome outfit with a standout colourful coat... or just go all out!

Ori photographed at home, London.

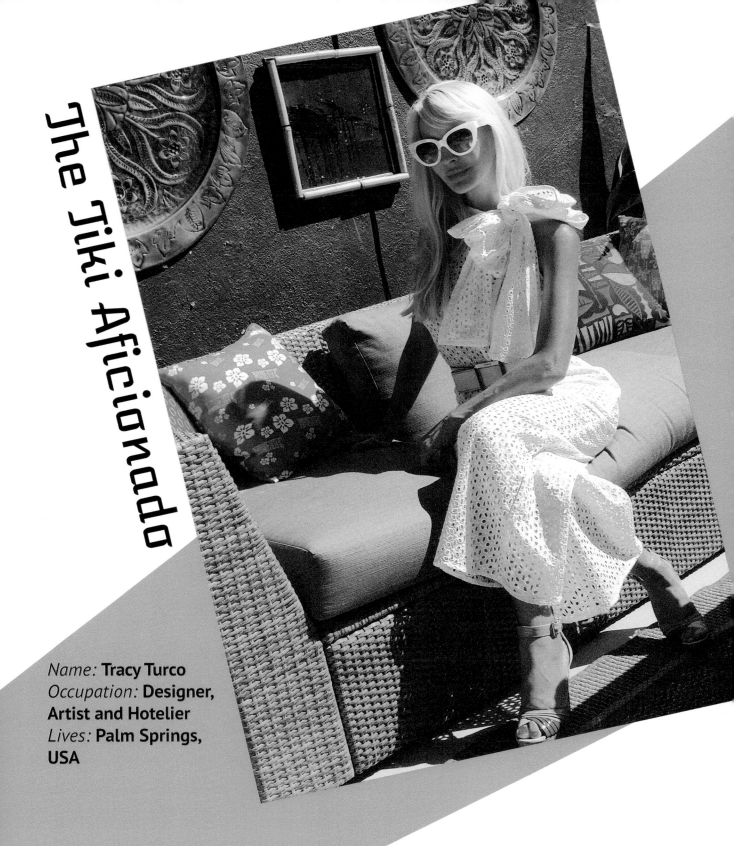

The Tiki Aficionado

Name: **Tracy Turco**
Occupation: **Designer, Artist and Hotelier**
Lives: **Palm Springs, USA**

Stepping into Tracy's Palm Springs home is like entering an immaculately preserved time machine. The designer's condo home is a homage to bold patterns and prints of the late-60s/early-70s interiors, with a heavy dose of tropical Tiki thrown in.

Tiki culture became all the rage in the 1930s, inspired by an idealised image of the South Pacific regions and the opening of Polynesian bars such as Don's Beachcomber. It peaked during the 50s and 60s, with the official Hawaiian statehood and Elvis' *Blue Hawaii* movie, and has since had various kitschy revivals, including Tiki cocktails becoming popular in the hipster craft cocktail scene.

Businesswoman and designer Tracy, who previously ran a successful tea company, has created a playful home that is all about escapism, making it the perfect fit for its Palm Springs location, in America's leisure capital.

Tracy photographed at home, Palm Springs.

What brought you to Palm Springs?

I've been coming to the area for about five years, as I have a geodesic dome in Joshua Tree. Then my husband and I started coming to Palm Springs and he just fell in love with the architecture, because when he was growing up his mom adored the Modernist era, especially architects like Frank Lloyd Wright. We went on some of the Old Hollywood tours and I really romanticize the Rat Pack era, so when we saw this house I just had to live here.

Palm Springs is a very different animal to New York. I really enjoy the whole vintage lifestyle – I still use a record player, I read books, and I'm not very good at social media! The Palm Springs lifestyle makes me feel younger than ever. We wake up in the morning and get on a bicycle to get coffee, which is unheard of! My kids laugh at us that we're riding bikes.

We are also currently opening up two new hotels in Palm Springs. My husband is in real estate development, so every property that we buy, I will design. One is called The Art Hotel, which will be like stepping back in time with retro-inspired interiors, and there's also a Tiki hotel.

Could you tell us about how you designed the interior of your house?

I was born in the 70s and still remember my parents having the dreaded avocado kitchen! I know this style is ugly, but to me it's ugly-fun.

In total, it took me about a year to design the interiors of this house. The interiors are an amalgamation of everything I can get my hands on. Garage sales, antique stores around the Palm Springs neighbourhood, malls, and overstocked.com. The fabric on all the pillows and duvets is from my own line at Society Six. The lights and the owls are all true vintage. The owners of the antique stores will call me to say they've got another owl in!

How would you describe your style fashion-wise?

My style is offbeat and ever changing. Think Ginger Grant from *Gilligan's Island* meets Farrah Fawcett from *Charlie's Angels*, with a little *Brady Bunch* mixed in, plus a slice of Slim Aarons' famous *Poolside Gossip* photo.

Where do you source your clothing? Is it mostly original vintage or reproduction, and are there any labels you particularly love?

Since high school, I have been collecting vintage pieces from labels such as Hattie Carnegie, Miriam Haskell, Stanley Hagler and Chanel. Over the years, I have found museum-quality gems from Halston, YSL and Elsa Schiaparelli hats, in their original boxes.

Before marriage, I was jet-setting across the world with my tea stores and would find inspiration in places like London, Paris, Russia, Berlin, China and Dubai. Now, when I'm in Palm Springs I shop for original vintage at the Palm Springs Vintage Market and Iconic Atomic, or Trina Turk for modern pieces with a retro style. I'm thinking of opening my own shop in Palm Springs with my favourite bits of vintage, and my own line of designer cabana wear inspired by poolside glamour and my love for all things Tiki.

What is it about the 60s and 70s that appeals?

I find this time to have been the most stylish era, eclectically mixing casual bohemian with glamorous disco. Fashion-wise, I love the ruffles, tall boots, dramatic capes and sparkling jumpsuits. My style icons of the time are Jimi Hendrix, Twiggy, Jane Birkin, plus designers André Courrèges, Ossie Clark and Pierre Cardin, and of course Andy Warhol and his factory.

The Vintage Historian

Name: **Amber Butchart**
Age: **38**
Occupation: **Fashion Historian, Author, Broadcaster & Lecturer**
Lives: **Margate, UK**

Amber is a Margate-based fashion historian, specialising in the relationship between clothing, culture and politics. She's worked in the fashion industry for years, as a buyer, writer and then BBC broadcaster, and her wealth of fashion knowledge means that she's so well versed in the fashion rules, she can break them with confidence.

Her wardrobe is an eclectic mix of eras and styles, and her magpie eye extends to the décor of her apartment, which is a treasure trove of antique finds and individual touches – such as the hand-painted tiles in the kitchen, created by her illustrator boyfriend Rob Flowers.

How would you describe your style?

Pat Butcher meets the art teacher in *Ghost World*.

Which is your favoured style era and what is it about this period that appeals?

My job involves researching clothing throughout history and I take inspiration from everything I explore, so it's very hard for me to choose just one era. But moments I return to are the 1920s, 1960s, and menswear in the 1780s – I love a breeches and stockings look.

What triggered your interest in historical dress and could you tell us a little about your career?

I always loved second-hand clothes as I was growing up. My mum mainly shopped in charity shops when I was younger, and the thrill of the hunt has stayed with me ever since. It's the stories that you can tell through old clothes that really fascinate me – I think it's a great window into history.

I began my career as the head buyer for a vintage clothing company, so the love of second-hand style became intrinsic to my livelihood from then onwards. The BBC TV series I made, *A Stitch in Time*, explored historical figures through the clothes they wore – so I got to dress up like Charles II and Marie Antoinette, amongst others!

Where do you get your style inspiration?

I'm always researching different periods of fashion history, so my inspiration largely comes from my work. I also spend a lot of time in museums, so I'd recommend a trip to the Fashion & Textile Museum or the V&A in London. On top of that, old films have always been a source of inspiration since I was a child.

Who are your style icons?

Marlene Dietrich, Quentin Crisp, Chimamanda Ngozi Adichie, Vesta Tilley and Liberace.

Is your wardrobe entirely original vintage or do you mix much repro and contemporary clothing in?

Not all my clothes are old but a lot of them are second hand. I often buy contemporary clothing in charity shops as well. I try to buy second hand as much as I can, but new clothing is sometimes a necessity, especially for tights – a staple of my wardrobe – and other basics.

Do you alter or make any of your own clothing?

I used to alter a lot of my clothing, but now if anything needs adjusting I take it to my dry cleaner. I did a pattern-cutting course after I left university, but I've never been very good at it!

Amber photographed at home, Margate.

Within the fashion industry, do you feel that there is a movement away from fast fashion?

Yes definitely. People – within the industry and some consumers – are beginning to realise that the way we buy and make clothing now is just not sustainable. Fashion is one of the most polluting industries on the planet. Fast fashion as a system is also beset with ethical issues from sweatshop production to murky supply chains and designer burn out. It takes a huge toll on the world.

Is sustainability a factor in your style choices, and if so how is this factored in?

It is a factor in that buying second hand is better than buying new, which is one of the reasons I try to shop second hand as much as possible. However, charity shops come with their own set of issues when they meet the global rag trade. I explored this in a documentary for BBC Radio 4, *From Rags to Riches*, which looked at the transition from 'second hand' to 'vintage' and also at the international

ramifications of our cast-off clothes. Sadly it's very difficult in the systems we live in to shop entirely ethically and sustainably.

Beyond how you dress, what other parts of your life are affected by your interest in period costume?

I'm half of a DJ duo called the Broken Hearts, and for over a decade we've been playing music from jump jive to calypso at parties around the world, so I'm definitely passionate about old music too. We used to co-host a weekly radio show on Jazz FM that focused on swing and early jazz, looking at the social history behind the tunes. My interiors aesthetic is also influenced by the past. I love bright colour and pattern everywhere, I wouldn't want to live with white walls. We have dead-stock late-1960s wallpaper in our flat, which has quite a mid-century baroque feel!

What is the future of fashion?

As a historian I'm more comfortable thinking about the past than the future. But the way we consume fashion now is not sustainable. The industry needs much more regulation from governments around the world.

The Fashion Archaeologist

Name:
Nicola Brierley
Occupation: **Owner of Little Sister vintage shop**
Lives: **London, UK**

Nicola has been in the vintage clothing business for over a decade, honing her eye for fashion gems. She's part of an entrepreneurial collective of Peckham business owners, who are injecting this South London area with creative shops and on-trend restaurants and bars, often in former disused buildings.

Nicola is the proud owner of Little Sister, a small destination boutique crammed with carefully sourced vintage from the 30s to the 90s. Her customers come not just for the clothing, but also to discover the narrative woven into each vintage piece. Nicola collects stories of the garment's former lives and passes it onto her customers, creating a truly personal connection between the clothing and its wearer.

What do you enjoy about selling vintage clothing?

I love the fact that I work in an industry where everything has a history, so you're never very far away from the past. I enjoy dissecting the past through clothing. It's interesting, for example, that you can't really find a lot of clothes from after the 1990s in the UK, which is linked to the industrial history and manufacturing stopping and going overseas under Thatcherism.

I also like that I do something that helps the environment and gives clothes a new lease of life.

Where are you sourcing clothing?

I go to car boot sales, charity shops or people might call me up if someone has passed away, been divorced or have just lost weight. You have to be very respectful looking at people's vintage, as you might not love it but it has its own history and energy. It's a very delicate and almost physiological thing to enter someone's space and look through their things.

I love it when I discover the history of the owner – perhaps they were an actress or they used to make their own clothes – it's those stories that resonate and my customers really want to know the background of each item. I also sell my own clothing here, and I love that a young person can wear that piece that always made me feel wonderful, and give it a new life.

Is sustainability a factor in your love for vintage?

Fashion is one of the biggest polluters and this can't continue. There is so much dead stock out there and we now have a six-week cycle of new clothing coming out. It's like a constant need to be fed – it's relentless.

With sustainability, it's something that has become important with everyone else but it's the way I've always lived my life. I was brought up this way – we used to go to Bell Street Market with my grandma and buy second-hand goods for the house – it was just the way we lived. Growing up, I never had the feeling that second hand was second best. It was an exciting experience but it was also because we didn't have any money. We might buy the functional things like shoes new, but the things we wanted for joy, or the high-fashion replicas, we had to buy these second hand. Even as my mum became more affluent, she'd still shop like that. My mum now lives in The States and we always go to thrift stores and flea markets there.

I'd encourage people to start buying vintage and put it back into the circular economy, so you wear it for a bit, then you sell it. In fact, people have sold my stuff back to me – they wore it for a couple of years then decided they don't love it any more so they sell it back or swap it.

How did Little Sister start?

For about ten years I had a shop on eBay and was a power seller for years. Then eBay changed the way you sell and introduced a 14-day return policy, which impacted vintage sellers as people could wear and return, which became like free hire.

I'd started to notice the lack of personal interaction – you don't get that online and it's very lonely. So I started to do more vintage fairs and enjoyed meeting people. I named the shop after Sly & The Family Stone, who had a record label named Little Sister. I've been here just over three years, and I'm really happy with my little space.

How would you describe your personal style?

It's eccentric and I'm constantly changing, as I'm easily bored. I don't wear one decade, I mix lots of different eras. I change my clothes and my hair entirely about once every three months.

How to breathe new life into clothing? Do you think being able to alter and mend your clothing is essential?

Learn how to mend your clothes – even the high street can one day become vintage if you know how to look after it. If you can't sew, then find yourself a good tailor.

Be careful and forensic when you buy something that needs mending – you can do things like invisible stitching, but unless you really love something, it will probably just sit there dead. People are now paying thousands of pounds to wear something that looks distressed – just buy vintage and you've got it for a fraction of the price.

Wash clothes on the lowest setting and not too often. As soon as you buy something vintage, put it in a bag and freeze it – which will get rid of all the moths and insects and extend the life of your clothes. Freeze it for three days, then shake it out and hang. A friend who works at the Victoria & Albert Museum told me that they use this technique for their archive clothing.

Is the vintage scene becoming more diverse?

The vintage scene is very female-led and there's a real support for our sisters, regardless of their ethnicity or country of origin. I don't see many black people working in vintage, but the ones I do see in London are really good, which excites me. There are a lot of mothers doing this, who are their own bosses. In terms of ageism, you can do this at any age – it's a good space for women to run their own businesses and do it successfully.

The people who buy vintage are also really diverse. You get the whole world coming to you, so it's an educational journey. I'm not only learning about the clothes, I'm learning about the people.

The 80s Peacock

Name:
Sarah Beetson
Age: **38**
Occupation: **Artist
and Illustrator**
Lives: **Australia**

Sarah photographed at Vintage by
the Sea Festival, Morecambe.

Any child of the 80s will be familiar with Sarah's retro inspirations, which include the tear-jerking *E.T.* epic, the *Star Wars* franchise, Madonna's club-kid look and the outrageously colourful Nerds candy sweets. A love for all things 80s has recently peaked, helped by nostalgic television shows such as *Stranger Things* and The Breakfast Club café in London, which serves up all the sugar-laden cereals of the decade.

It's no coincidence that we are now, 30-odd years later, looking back at the decade of the 80s with a misty eye, as this ties in neatly with American film critic Lindsay Ellis' notion of the 30-year cycle. Ellis notes that the media is prone to idealising the period around 30 years previous, as the people who were consumers of culture as children have now become creators of culture as adults. Just look at 80s hit films such as *Dirty Dancing* and *Back to the Future*, which offered a sanitised version of the 50s.

We're currently in the midst of a pop culture fascination with the 80s and 90s, having been able to distance ourselves with enough time to look back and cherry-pick the references that hold an emotional connection, without feeling the frustrations of the era that a shorter refection period might have produced. In the world of vintage nostalgia, what comes around goes around, and it's usually around 30 years afterwards apparently.

How would you describe your style?

All colour, all the time.

Do you dress this way everyday?

Yes, except during yoga classes, and when I'm actually painting I wear jeans and vintage tees that double as paintbrush cloths, hence they are covered in a rainbow palette of paint!

Are environmental concerns a factor in wearing vintage?

Yes, very much so. I try to buy from charity shops, which we call op shops in Australia. I do peruse vintage stores on my travels in the UK and US – though if they are very overpriced I will make a sneaky list in my phone of my favourite finds and search them out on eBay or Etsy for a fraction of the price. This is particularly handy for 80s vintage band and tour tees!

Where do you get your style inspiration?

I think my biggest early influence came from the 80s band Guns N' Roses. I'm also obsessed with cowboy boots, military hats and jackets – and a good dose of that comes from Michael Jackson and Madonna in the same era. I'm in love with sports and leisurewear, circa 1977–1985.

I think my style was really formed working at the London punk club The Electric Ballroom in the early 2000s, when you could still pick all of that stuff up for fairly cheap. I also have a thing for skirts made from recycled 80s kids movie, cartoon and comic sheets, curtains and duvet covers – some of my wardrobe staples are the from the movies *Star Wars*, *Return of the Jedi*, *Masters of the Universe*, *The Phantom*, *E.T.* and *An American Tail*, plus Nerds candy. My other style icons are Anna Piaggi, Iris Apfel, Divine, The New York Dolls, Billy Idol and Prince.

Where do you source your clothing and accessories?

For fair prices, I love Beyond Retro in London and Search and Destroy on St Marks Place, NYC. I also try to buy from friends in fashion, for example Captain Robbo in Melbourne creates hand screen-printed cotton leggings in colourful prints. I also utilize my own illustration work as pattern repeats which I will print in small runs and ask fashion designer friends to sew into clothes for me.

And independent boutiques are my favourite – I recently visited I Need More in New York's Lower East Side and met owner and founder of Trash and Vaudeville Jimmy Webb, who calls Iggy Pop, Slash and Debbie Harry friends! His boutique stocks amazing rock-star-worthy sequinned, hand-painted leather jackets and some of the lushest hand-made punk items you could wish to find.

Other shops I love include Affleck's in Manchester. As a teenager in the late 90s I used to love sourcing their 70s Adidas zip-ups for £5, but I'm not sure it's still as great as it once was. RetroStar in Melbourne is amazing. Search and Destroy in New York is amazing for vintage punk – they have a lot of old stage items and props from CBGBs in there. I bought a denim jacket from there covered in patches from every tourist attraction in DC, Ohio and Pennsylvania that was once owned by a teenage boy named Craig – I know this because his name is scrawled on the collar!

Beyond the dress, which other aspects of your life are affected by your interest in vintage?

My artwork is undoubtedly influenced by the same era and sensibilities as my personal style. I am obsessed by cult movies from the 70s, 80s and 90s and have devoted entire art series to them. My art heroes tend to be from my favourite vintage eras too – film director John Waters, photographer Martin Parr, illustrator Antonio Lopez, fashion designer John Galliano, writer Richard Brautigan, singer PJ Harvey and movies including *Flashdance* and the kids from *Fame*.